A CLOUD BY DAY,
A FIRE BY NIGHT

Books by A.W. Tozer

A CLOUD BY DAY,
A FIRE BY NIGHT

▼

Finding and Following God's Will for You

A.W. TOZER

COMPILED AND EDITED BY JAMES L. SNYDER

BETHANY HOUSE
a division of Baker Publishing Group
Minneapolis, Minnesota

© 2019 by James L. Snyder

Published by Bethany House Publishers
11400 Hampshire Avenue South
Minneapolis, Minnesota 55438
www.bethanyhouse.com

Bethany House Publishers is a division of
Baker Publishing Group, Grand Rapids, Michigan

Printed in the United States of America

Library of Congress Cataloging-in-Publication Data
Names: Tozer, A. W. (Aiden Wilson), 1897–1963, author. | Snyder, James L., editor.
Title: A cloud by day, a fire by night : finding and following God's will for you /
    A.W. Tozer ; compiled and edited by James L. Snyder.
Description: Minneapolis : Bethany House Publishers, a division of Baker
    Publishing Group, 2019. | Tozer's teachings on God's will taken from his
    sermons. | Includes bibliographical references.
Identifiers: LCCN 2018042245| ISBN 9780764218095 (pbk. : alk. paper) | ISBN
    9781493417155 (e-book)
Subjects: LCSH: God (Christianity)—Will—Sermons. | Providence and government
    of God—Christianity—Sermons.
Classification: LCC BT135 .T69 2019 | DDC 248.4—dc23
LC record available at https://lccn.loc.gov/2018042245

Scripture quotations are from the King James Version of the Bible.

Cover design by Rob Williams, InsideOutCreativeArts

James L. Snyder is represented by The Steve Laube Agency.

Baker Publishing Group publications use paper produced from sustainable forestry practices and post-consumer waste whenever possible.

22 23 24 25 26 27 28   10 9 8 7 6 5 4

Contents

*And the Lord went before them by day in a
pillar of a cloud, to lead them the way; and
by night in a pillar of fire, to give them light;
to go by day and night: He took not away
the pillar of the cloud by day, nor the pillar of fire by night, from before the people.*

Exodus 13:21–22

*Behold, I send an Angel before thee, to keep
thee in the way, and to bring thee into the
place which I have prepared.*

Exodus 23:20

Introduction

A very important theme in Dr. A.W. Tozer's ministry was the subject of God's will for each of our lives. He wrestled with it from the time he was a new Christian until the day he passed into eternity.

This book, drawn from a sermon series Dr. Tozer delivered just before leaving his successful church in Chicago, is not a manual on how to find God's will for your life in five easy steps. Tozer abhorred that sort of thing. There's no such thing as "easy steps" in discovering God's will for your life.

When Tozer preached these sermons, the people of Southside Alliance didn't know his plans, but certain developments were leading Tozer to end his thirty years at Southside and accept a call to pastor a church in Toronto. I'm sure he wrestled with the decision for a long time.

The series, titled "An Angel before Thee," also holds significance because Tozer shared a number of personal stories, including how God led him from Indianapolis, where he was a successful pastor, to Southside Alliance, which was rather new at the time.

Central to Tozer's teaching is what he liked to call the deeper life. This is a life that is spiritually deeper than the average Christian's. He bemoans the downgrading of Christianity. The Christianity he was committed to is a progressive upgrading of our walk with Jesus Christ.

Tozer believed that living the Christian life is more than being saved by God and then waiting to go to heaven. Several times he would tell his Chicago congregation something like, "If everyone today were physically what they were spiritually, many of you would be wearing diapers and sucking your thumbs." It always got a laugh, but he had a point.

Throughout this book he discusses the battles Christians face almost every day. He frames these battles as taking place in Canaan, as he calls it—the land of promise where we are living today. There are some who dismiss the idea that a Christian will face battles or need spiritual warfare. Yet the reality is we all experience battles according to the level of our progress in Canaan. In chapter 15, Tozer shows the connection between battles and blessings. He points out that you can't have a blessing until you have experienced a battle. But the purpose of the battle is to get us to the blessing. Tozer explores another seeming dichotomy in chapter 22, where he talks about the benefits that can come from discouragement. Only Tozer could look at something so negative and find positives from a spiritual point of view.

Anybody who has ever listened to one of Dr. Tozer's sermons knows of his great love for hymns. Each chapter begins with a prayer by Tozer and concludes with a verse or two from a hymn that reflects that chapter's topic.

The primary thing I believe Tozer would want the reader to get out of this book is simply this: Never give up; never quit.

So much in life can bring us to that point of discouragement where all we want to do is quit, especially when God's will for us is unclear. For Tozer, quitting was not an option. You will read how, as a young man, Tozer felt God's leading to become a pastor. He lacked the typical qualifications an ordination committee would require, but he was determined and had faith that it was God's will. He learned years later that many of the committee members did indeed question his qualifications, but they also saw his heart for ministry and made ordination possible. I love that story.

This book is about more than finding God's will for your next step or decision in life—it is about following His will to the end. With only our human resources, following God would be impossible. But when we cross that line into the deeper life, we enter into the grace of God that enables us to do His will.

1

Seeking Direction

Heavenly Father, I come before Thee yearning to know and desiring to trust Thee. May my heart be open to whatever Thou hast for me so I can be where Thou wants me to be. May I yield to Thine Angel before me and come to the place Thou desirest for me. Keep me under the cloud by day and the fire by night. In Jesus' name, amen.

Thirty-two years ago, at a crucial and painful hour in my life, God began speaking to me about His will for me. I had been the pastor of the Christian and Missionary Alliance church in Indianapolis for several years, and God was blessing and using me in wonderful ways. The church was growing and making an impact on the community, and I had no desire whatsoever to leave Indianapolis.

Then I began getting letters from the Christian and Missionary Alliance church in Chicago inviting me to candidate to be their next pastor. I had no interest in moving and threw the letters away. Yet God began speaking to me about Chicago, though I wasn't sure why. Finally, I decided I would go to preach there on a Sunday, but pastoring the church was out of the question. Like Calvin Coolidge once famously pronounced, I informed the good people there after preaching, "I do not choose to run."

But driving back to Indianapolis I found myself in an agony of heart-searching prayer. God was speaking to my heart, and I did not know what I was to do. I truly was in a spiritual dilemma.

When God speaks to us, He does so in a way that opens up to us His plan for our lives. I thought God's plan for me was to stay in Indianapolis. Everything was going great. The church was growing, and our influence was felt throughout the city.

That morning in Chicago I preached on Exodus 23:20: "Behold, I send an Angel before thee, to keep thee in the way, and to bring thee into the place which I have prepared." I understood the primary historical meaning of the passage. Certainly I could preach a sermon on the passage and then walk away.

God, however, would not allow it.

I saw and felt the Scripture's direct meaning for me. God was speaking to me, a spiritual son of Abraham, from His covenant with Abraham. The spiritual laws were in effect and God was reaching out to me in this. It was applicable to me as an individual, but also to the church in their earthly pilgrimage.

I firmly believe that God is speaking today to the church at large and giving us commands based on His covenant with Abraham. God is directing His people in the way He wants them to go. Often it is not the way we want to go, but as we yield ourselves to God, He opens doors and leads us forward. And so the church's responsibility is to hear that voice and then obey that voice.

After more heart-searching prayer, I finally decided to accept the pastorate in Chicago. It was a big change for me. The church was relatively new, with little heritage to speak of. I came in as a country boy and began my ministry in the big city.

I am here to testify that when God spoke to me about Chicago and I responded in the affirmative, He fulfilled His covenant with me in spite of my personal failures. I will be the first to acknowledge that I have had many failures. You cannot live very long and not accumulate them. But in His graciousness, God uses us, failures and all, in such a way that He receives glory.

God has been moving in our congregation and opening up opportunities for us to fulfill His will in our lives. Nearly twenty-five young people have gone out as missionaries, serving the Lord Jesus Christ. Another ten or so have become pastors and preachers, and our congregation has encouraged them to fulfill God's calling on their lives. In addition, we have a large number of musicians and music directors and home missionaries. I also rejoice in how God has been financially blessing our interest in foreign missions, stirring our hearts to give sacrificially unto Him.

In His graciousness, God uses us, failures and all, in such a way that He receives glory.

When we allow God's Word to go beyond our ears and into our hearts, it stimulates us to do that which God is calling us to do.

Every one of us will face challenges in life, individually and in our churches. Our congregation is being affected by the steady trend of industry and people moving to the suburbs. The neighborhood has deteriorated around us, and crime is making it hard to have any kind of an evening service. The crippling of our public transportation system has also kept many people from coming to our church. None of these things could have been foreseen twenty years ago. Our focus was and is on obeying God and responding to His voice.

Travelers going through an unfamiliar land need to hear a clear word—a voice of wisdom—to guide them. Otherwise they will wander in a hopeless sense of lostness.

To avoid wrong turns, we need to base every decision on the authority and wisdom of God's Word. My aim for this book is to help us understand this clear word from God. What is God saying? Where can I hear this voice that's going to give me direction throughout my life?

It is the voice of God that will guide our way through our personal Jordan rivers and into the promised land. Without that voice of God, our Jordan will never open up, and we will never get across.

Guide Me, O Thou Great Jehovah

Guide me, O Thou great Jehovah,
Pilgrim through this barren land;
I am weak, but Thou art mighty,
Hold me with Thy pow'rful hand.
Bread of heaven, bread of heaven,
Feed me till I want no more;
Feed me till I want no more.

William Williams (1717–1791)

2

The Unmistakable Voice of God

Heavenly Father, the greatest desire in my heart is to hear from Thee. Not simply to hear about Thee, but to hear Thy unmistakable voice resonate within my heart, calling me to a stance of obedience before Thee. Hear me, O Father, so I may hear that unmistakable voice of Thine. I pray this in Jesus' name, amen.

With all kinds of voices in the world, we are often caught up in those voices instead of God's. Even when He calls out "Behold!" to get our attention, we can miss out because we have surrounded ourselves with things and activities that drown out the voice of God.

I suggest we push those extra things out of our lives so we can hear the still, small, most mighty voice of God.

God takes the initiative to provide direction for your life. In the Scripture we are studying, Exodus 23:20–23, He promises, "I send an Angel before thee." He will not let us flounder on our own. Rather, He will send an Angel to guide us.

The Lord also takes responsibility "to keep thee in the way" (v. 20). He sends an Angel before us so that we know which way to go amid life's many distractions. Even apparent opportunities may turn out to be distractions if they are not God's will. So this Angel is to keep us in the way He wants us to go.

God also promises "to bring thee into the place" (v. 20). This is crucial. God begins our journey, and the Angel knows the way; only He can take us to the place of God's choosing. God's wisdom opens up divine opportunities for us. We may not recognize it in the moment, but there will be an inner voice that speaks confidently, "This is the way, walk ye in it" (Isaiah 30:21).

Exodus 23:20 ends with "the place which I have prepared." God has already prepared the place where He wants us to go. Coming to Chicago, I really did not know that God had prepared Chicago for me and me for Chicago.

We need to relax a bit, turn away from the noise of the world, and listen to the voice of God because He has everything put together. He has prepared for us a place of service and ministry and will open the necessary doors, despite the obstacles and the confusion we may experience during the journey.

I need to quiet my heart in order to hear God's direction. This must become a daily discipline for all of us. It is too easy and convenient to trust human inclinations. We gravitate toward earthly methods. We want human understanding. As a culture, we have become addicted to devices and technology. However, those who refuse to trust in these human inclinations and devices are the ones who have their ears open to hear the voice of the Lord.

We must also have a desire to enter God's prepared place. That's where I want to go. I think all of us who have been born again and love the Lord Jesus Christ should want to go to that place God has prepared for us—the ministry He has laid out for us. We may not know what that is initially. It may seem ambiguous, but we need to trust that God knows what He's doing and is going to lead us through our Jordan.

I knew what my ministry was in Indianapolis. When God called me to Chicago, I didn't have a vision for ministry there. Indianapolis and Chicago are different cities and demand different ministries. I did not know that until I got there.

Those who are willing to go God's way want to hear the voice of God. The voice of man goes this way and that, but God's way is always the best. When I surrender myself to God, when I accept nothing less than God's way revealed to me through God's voice, I will get to the place He wants me to be.

Having faith to follow God's leading isn't easy. We may encounter a great deal of difficulties—difficulties we didn't anticipate. There will be times we want to quit. But those of us who put our faith and trust in Jesus Christ need to realize that no matter how terrible our circumstances, or how the enemy may come against us, we should have faith in the God who is leading us. That Angel set before us is God's appointed one. He will lead us through our Jordan to where God can be glorified through our ministry.

The voice of man goes this way and that, but God's way is always the best.

Think of the people who will come to Christ when we follow this Angel. Think of those who will respond to God's calling and enter a ministry of God's choosing.

You may see challenges before you, but no challenge is bigger than God. Not one challenge could ever surprise God in the least. When we start our journey with God, He knows the beginning and the end and everything in between. His preparation in us is in complete harmony with His knowledge of everything that is going to happen to us. Nothing can ever happen to you or me but what God has prepared us to handle.

This Angel before us is faithfully leading us to the place where God wants us to be.

The Voice of God Is Calling

The voice of God is calling
   its summons in our day;
Isaiah heard in Zion,
   and we now hear God say:
"Whom shall I send to succor
   my people in their need?
Whom shall I send to loosen
   the bonds of shame and greed?"

John Haynes Holmes
(1879–1964)

3

The Focus on
Our Final Destination

▼

Heavenly Father, with great earnestness of heart, I beseech Thee to enable me to put my focus where Thou wants it to be. Not on this life. Not on the things around me. But, O God, may my focus be completely upon Thee and what Thou hast for me. I know this life has a limit to it. I also know the destination Thou hast for me is that eternity without any kind of limitation where I will enjoy a relationship with Thee that I can't enjoy right now. I look forward to that final destination. Gratefully in Jesus' name, amen.

Leading God's people out of Egypt and into the promised land demanded a uniquely called person. Moses was God's solution to Israel's problem.

Whenever there is a problem or difficult situation, God always brings in a person with His anointing to solve it. Look at all of the prophets throughout the Old Testament, and you will see how God works. I must say, though, that it's disappointing how many times the prophets were rejected by the people they were trying to help. This goes on today as well.

We know the story of Israel wandering in the wilderness for forty years before getting into the land God promised them. Israel rejected the leadership of Moses and turned their back on the promised land.

This ancient journey, this experience of wandering, is an illustration of the Christian walk today from earth to heaven. Paul says, "Now all these things happened unto them for examples: and they are written for our admonition, upon whom the ends of the world are come" (1 Corinthians 10:11).

God is going to lead us to His promised land, a land we can't even imagine at this point. The journey begins with our conversion and progresses through obstacles toward a victorious, fruitful life in the Lord Jesus Christ. But again, we are not alone in our journey, for God has appointed an Angel before us to guide us in the way He has prepared.

I think we are, therefore, in accord with people like the apostle Paul. Look at his testimony and how God started with him on the road to Damascus. From there, it was a journey with all kinds of obstacles on either side of the pathway. But Paul endured it all because he was following the voice of God. His path led him to being martyred, but that, you can be sure, was not the end of the apostle Paul.

Consider the apostle John in the book of Revelation and all he experienced. His vision of heaven motivated him and his ministry even though it cost him greatly.

Read about the church fathers and how they were chosen by God and how God directed them and led many of them also to martyrdom. They were the reformers, the mystics, and so forth. Not only did God guide them, but He set them as examples for us to follow.

I want to look more closely at the divine declaration that we are going to the place God has prepared. Everything God is doing directs us to that predetermined destination. He is systematically preparing us in this life for that place, and our obedience to God now will be reflected in our position in heaven.

There are two sides to this: provisional destinations and our final destination.

In Deuteronomy 1:30 we read, "The Lord your God which goeth before you, he shall fight for you, according to all that he did for you in Egypt before your eyes." God has a final destination for Israel, but in between are steps—layers of conflict and battles—but He promises Israel He will go before them and fight their battles for them. Every step of the way has been set by God, and one step leads to the next.

Rarely do we see many steps ahead of us. We need to walk entirely by faith. But like God did for Israel, He prepares us for one step at a time. The pathway is of His choosing and may not match the way we want. But to overstep God's plan is disaster. As a Christian, I go forward under the power of the Holy Spirit, who is leading and preparing me for the path chosen for me.

I believe this also applies to the local church. If we are open to the Holy Spirit, He will lead us on the pathway—a destiny and a ministry He has in mind for us. At this point we may not fully know what that ministry is. We may not know where we are going, but as long as we are following the Lord, we have nothing to fear. As we let go of our past, we can get a firm grip on the future God has for us.

Then we come to the Lord's final destination for us. For Israel, this was the point of full possession of Canaan. God used Moses to lead them out of Egypt and into the wilderness, and Joshua finally led them across the Jordan River and into the promised land.

> *We may not know where we are going, but as long as we are following the Lord, we have nothing to fear.*

Our final destination is "my Father's house," Jesus says in John 14:2. This world is not our home or our final destination. Our path has been engineered by God, and He leads by no other way. Many get sidetracked by the world, and unfortunately, they do not reach the place God has for them.

The Christian's destination is fruitfulness and power along the way and, finally, heaven. As we go along God's path, we will find all the provisions we need to be who God wants us to be so that we can arrive at the place God has prepared for us. By faith, each day we access God's provision for us.

We never know what we will need, but God does and has made full provision.

To reach that place requires a power not equal but superior to the opposition. We need to always keep that in mind. It is so easy to get diverted from the path the Angel has set before us. But God is providing a cloud by day and a fire by night in order to get us to our destination.

▼

When the Roll Is Called Up Yonder

When the trumpet of the Lord shall sound, and time
    shall be no more,
And the morning breaks, eternal, bright and fair;
When the saved of earth shall gather over on the
    other shore,
And the roll is called up yonder, I'll be there.

James M. Black (1856–1938)

4

Trusting the Holy Spirit to Lead Us

▼

O gracious Father, Thy guidance in my life is so greatly needed and appreciated. When I try on my own, I only fail. The work of the Holy Spirit in my life is guiding me to the destination Thou hast established. May I be faithful, God, to Thy leadership. May those around me see Thy work in me. In Jesus' name, amen.

Who is this angelic messenger God sends before us? I believe we have here an illustration, or symbol, of the Holy Spirit. God, the Holy Spirit, is guiding us and directing us to the place of His choosing. We need to surrender to Him, we need to know who this Holy Spirit is, and we need to get to the point of trusting Him in our day-to-day decisions. If we are to get to where God wants us, we must fully accept His provisions along the way. This Holy Spirit is God's omniscient providence and provision for us.

Consider some of the attributes of this Angel. In Exodus 23:21 we read, "Beware of him, and obey his voice, provoke him not; for he will not pardon your transgressions: for my name is in him."

I want to point out here that this Angel cannot lead an enemy. That is not His purpose. He is not leading the enemy to where God wants them to be. God has given Him no authority over the enemy. That's something we need to grasp ahold of.

He also has no authority to overlook stubbornness, rebellion, unbelief, or disobedience in us. He has to deal with all of these things, which is why the Scripture says, "beware of him."

He has what is needed to bring us to and keep us on the right path.

The relationship of a physician with his patient would be a good illustration of this. The physician must have cooperation. If the patient is fighting against the doctor, the doctor cannot do what needs to be done for the patient. It is when the patient surrenders to the doctor that he gets the help he needs.

If we are fighting against God, if we are overlooking the leadership of God through this Angel before us, we are not going to get very far. The path before us is of such a nature that we cannot navigate it on our own—we need a guide.

This Angel will not overlook anything; He is under divine orders and responds and reports to God, not to us. He is not at our dispatch. He is in our lives to fulfill God's purpose, not ours.

Of course, the question before us is, What if we sin? Like the prodigal son, if we acknowledge that we have sinned, we will find the forgiveness of God. Sin cannot keep us from God if we follow His voice and obey Him.

> *The Angel is not at our dispatch. He is in our lives to fulfill God's purpose, not ours.*

The history of Israel tells us that God did exercise forgiveness with them. One generation was walking where God wanted them to walk and was in the delight of God. The next generation made their own choices and consequently experienced the displeasure of God. For some reason they wanted to go their way instead of God's. "Every man did that which was right in his own eyes" (Judges 17:6).

We find this also in the New Testament. Churches started out going in the right direction, but soon they wanted to make their own decisions and go their own way. Most of Paul's epistles were directed to churches to stop this practice, turn around, and continue to follow the Lord Jesus

34

Christ. This happens today. We are trying to validate the culture around us so we can in good conscience pull it into the church.

Certainly sin will prevent us from going in God's direction, but this does not apply to sin repented of. That is the key. Sin was the great deterrent in Israel's history and in the church's history, and it is in our own histories as individual Christians as well. The imperfection of man did not come as a surprise to God. All of His plans have been put together with every contingency thought through, so when man fails, it is no surprise to God and He has a solution already in motion. If He had not included the potential for man's imperfection, His plans could only fail, and that is also unthinkable. Man's imperfections are proof of God's grace.

Think of Jacob and his failures. He probably had more failures than anybody else, but he repented and God restored him. It is the restoration of God that makes the difference in our lives. Jacob encountered that ladder to heaven, and it completely changed his life: "Surely the Lord is in this place; and I knew it not" (Genesis 28:16).

I read of Job in the Old Testament, where he says, "Behold, I am vile; what shall I answer thee? I will lay mine hand upon my mouth" (Job 40:4). But that was not his end. He went through insufferable difficulties, and nobody seemed to be on his side, not even his wife. When he says, "Though he slay me, yet will I trust in him" (Job 13:15), that is Job finding out that his imperfections did not matter when it came to following God. God could rise above all of the failures in his life.

The same is true of Elijah when he cries out to God, "Take away my life" (1 Kings 19:4). Later, there is the wonderful scene of the chariot escorting Elijah into heaven (2 Kings 2:11). Sure, Elijah had his problems, but an unrepentant heart was not one of them. He repented, turned to God, and gave God the opportunity to use him.

In the New Testament, there's the occasion when Peter said, "I know him not" (Luke 22:57), referring to Jesus. What a heartbreaking experience that must have been for Jesus. Peter spent all his time with Jesus, and when it really mattered, Peter denied the Lord. However, that was not the end of the story. Even though he denied the Lord, he turned his heart around, confessed his sin, repented, and was brought back into the leading position of the church at that time. It was Peter who preached at Pentecost, which began the move of the Holy Spirit that is active even today.

God's grace is not only for our imperfections and weaknesses and failures. His grace is a reflection of His character and His nature, not our weaknesses.

Meister Eckhart, the German theologian, wrote hundreds of years ago, "God does not look at what you do but only at your love and at the devotion and will behind your deeds. . . . He is concerned only that we shall love him in all things."[1]

Most importantly, the Bible records these words of Solomon: "I know that, whatsoever God doeth, it shall be for ever: nothing can be put to it, nor any thing taken from it: and God doeth it, that men should fear before him" (Ecclesiastes 3:14).

God waits for that moment when we repent of our sin and then experience the overwhelming sense of His forgiveness. No one can sin too much to receive God's mercy if he or she repents sincerely.

There's a Wideness in God's Mercy

There's a wideness in God's mercy,
like the wideness of the sea.
There's a kindness in God's justice,
which is more than liberty.
There is no place where earth's sorrows
are more felt than up in heaven.
There is no place where earth's failings
have such kindly judgment given.

Frederick William Faber
(1814–1863)

5

Unbelief vs. Belief

Our Father, I pray that I might repent before Thee. If I am preoccupied with earthly things, I repent of this. I would confess of my obsession with the things that pass away. O Lord, forgive me, cleanse me, wash me so that as I quiet my heart and in silence wait on Thee, I may receive as unworthy, but believing, that which Thou hast for me. I pray this in Jesus' holy name, amen.

n Exodus 23, God lays out before Moses spiritual laws necessary for Israel to go where God wants them to go. It is essential that we understand how those laws operate throughout the kingdom of God.

Keep in mind that God never changes, and neither do His laws. Of course, in the Old Testament the Jewish leaders layered the law with all kinds of extra laws that really did not enhance what God wanted them to do. In fact, it fogged up the whole picture and created a certain level of confusion.

Today we are guilty of that very thing. We have laws in our gospel churches that are in no way compatible with the laws God laid out for His kingdom. As a believer, my job is to seek God in His Word and strip from my life everything hindering my relationship with God. If we are going to accomplish God's goals, we need to get back to the basic laws of the kingdom of God laid out for us.

The first step is comprehending what unbelief does.

Unbelief hinders the operation of the spiritual laws, laws of the kingdom. If we do not believe God in everything, then we are hindering the laws of God as He intended them. This impedes our own spiritual progress. If we are not following the laws God has laid down for us and are following instead the laws man has laid down, we are compromising our progress and no longer going in the direction God wants us to go.

Unbelief also interferes with the Lord's leading. If I'm not believing God, I'm not being led by God. My unbelief will cloud what God wants to do in my life. That is the thing most important to many Christians who have been wandering aimlessly for too long and have become discouraged. We need to wake up to the call of God and the laws of the kingdom and get back to where God wants us to be.

How can we identify this term "unbelief"? People talk about belief and unbelief, and I would stress the truth that unbelief is found in the so-called church today. Unbelief hinders believers from the promises of God. If you asked them, they would agree with what God has said and claim to believe all of His promises. But unbelief says that this is for someone else, somewhere else, and at some other time. Unbelief deflects correction and says that it doesn't apply to me.

If I'm not believing God, I'm not being led by God.

Unbelief says, "Some other time, not now. Yes, that's what God says, but certain things have changed, so it doesn't really apply to us today." They believe in what God is saying, but not for right now.

Unbelief says, "Some other place, not here. Yes, I believe the promises of God, but they're not for here. We are living in a different place, and the promises of God do not really apply. It was good for Israel and Canaan, but I'm not in Canaan."

Unbelief says, "Someone else, not me. Yes, I believe the promises, but they really are not for me. Certain promises don't apply to me, so I can get out of obeying God's Word."

It would be hard to find someone who would say they did not believe the promises of God and the laws associated with the kingdom of God. They believe, but there is an element of unbelief in their life. Unbelief believes all of the promises conditionally for someone else, somewhere else, and at some other time. They believe what God says is true, but it isn't relevant to them at this time in their life.

Unfortunately, unbelief is carrying the day. In many gospel churches, it is the pattern many are following, which is the reason many are aimless and going nowhere as far as God's kingdom is concerned.

The question that desperately needs to be answered is, How does faith differ from unbelief?

The difference is simply that faith says, "If some other time, then why not now?" And that's the important thing. If God said it for some other time, why does it not apply now? Faith says emphatically that it does apply to me right now.

Faith also says, "If some other place, then why not right here? If it's good wherever, then why can't it be good here where I am standing?"

Faith says, "If someone else, then why not me? Whatever God has done for anybody else, God can do for me."

Faith takes the "I" out of the equation and brings God back to the center. If God said it, then it must be true, and if it's true, then it's true now, and if it's true for someone else, it's also true for me. Somehow, we have taken the Scripture and parsed it to mean "that one" when it means "this one."

We must recognize the difference between unbelief and belief. If we are going to follow this Angel before us, we need to know what God has in store for us. By trusting God whether we understand His plan or not, we are placing ourselves in the path where He can lead us to where He wants us to be.

Basically, there are two kinds of Christians: one who believes the truth and one who doesn't believe the truth. What a difference between the two.

There are weeds of unbelief choking our belief. Our job is to find them and uproot them from our lives. The Angel before me will faithfully lead me away from all elements of unbelief hiding within my life.

▼

Come, Thou Fount of Every Blessing

O to grace how great a debtor
    daily I'm constrained to be!
Let Thy goodness, like a fetter,
    bind my wandering heart to Thee:
Prone to wander, Lord, I feel it,
    prone to leave the God I love;
Here's my heart, O take and seal it,
    seal it for Thy courts above.

Robert Robinson (1735–1790)

6

God's Promise Is Contingent on Our Obedience

▼

O Son of God, most holy, born, crucified, risen, and coming again, we beseech Thee. Rebuke all the unholiness in our hearts and minds, all that is negative and hindering the operation of Thy Holy Spirit. O, let the Shekinah be seen today, and let it hover over each habitation showing that the Lord is God. Make us holy as Thou art holy and by surrender and faith, purify our hearts unto Thee. We beseech Thee to answer all this in Christ our Lord. Amen.

Obedience is the key aspect of my relationship with God. In Exodus 23:22 God says, "But if thou shalt indeed obey his voice, and do all that I speak; then I will be an enemy unto thine enemies, and an adversary unto thine adversaries."

This is the promise of God. If we obey His voice and do all He says, then He will be our strength and our foundation. This does not in any way disqualify people who have slipped or failed or lapsed or disobeyed. We all fail from time to time. The path back to the main path is one of confession and repentance. He is not disqualifying people for mistakes they make, but He is saying, "If you come back and obey My voice, then I will be your strength."

Our fall, our depravity, our weakness, and our flesh do not really disqualify us if we are listening to the voice of God, and in listening we are obeying. Obedience is always the key.

Our enemies are Satan and sin and the world around us. And if we are going to have victory over them, we cannot do it in our own strength because that's where we fall.

Even with all his deceptive abilities, Satan can never outwit God, even though he has tried since the beginning of time. Also, nothing man could ever do could enable him to outwit God. God is perfect in all His attributes, and everything God does He does in the essence of perfection and beauty and glory.

Israel never expected to enter the promised land unopposed. When they went into the promised land, the battles really began with opposition all along the way. Joshua led them to victory because God promised He would be an enemy to their enemies and an adversary to their adversaries.

We all fail from time to time . . . but God says, "If you come back and obey My voice, then I will be your strength."

I believe the same is true for us today. We cannot live the Christian life and expect we will never be opposed. There is so much opposition to Christianity in the world, and it has been that way since the beginning.

Read *Foxe's Book of Martyrs* and you will see how men and women of God were opposed violently by Satan and the world and everything around them.

In my Christian walk, if I am opposed and fade away, it's because I don't realize there will be opposition and that my real enemy is Satan. He works to oppose us at every level, and for the most part, I'm sad to say, he is successful. Satan through demons and other people and circumstances puts up opposition that is too strong for us alone. There is no way in our flesh we could ever stand against the enemy.

I would underscore that he cannot beat God at His game.

I think David understood this when he stood against Goliath. Goliath was the stronger of the two. There was no way this little boy, David, could ever defeat that enemy with a slingshot. But David came against Goliath not in his own strength but in the name of the Lord.

God identifies himself with us completely. God created us, God created everything around us, and God knows exactly what we are up against.

To avoid spiritual confusion, we need to understand the difference between an enemy and an adversary.

An enemy is one hostile toward us. This enemy, however, can be temporarily inactive. We can have an enemy out there, but he is not attacking or opposing us—he is just out there.

An adversary is different. An adversary is an enemy in active opposition. God has said if we follow Him our adversary will be His adversary. Although our adversary can overcome us, it can never overcome God. God stands strong, and when He faces our enemy there simply is no competition.

Our victory in the Christian experience rests upon our obedience. I can't stress too much how important it is to obey God. In order to obey God fully, we need to be saturated in the Word of God under the leadership of the Holy Spirit.

Many times in our daily walk we focus on an enemy. We have the right focus, but the enemy is dormant. We are satisfied with the fact that the enemy is not active. We do not give consideration to the fact that there is an adversary out there. That adversary is an enemy in action trying to defeat us.

My obedience is based on my commitment to God. As I understand my commitment to God, I begin to see flowing into my life the attributes of God that protect me from an enemy or an adversary.

Too often, I see Christians fighting enemies that are truly not our enemies. I see Christians fighting one another. My advice is simply that your enemy does not sit in the pew next to you.

By committing myself to God, I will certainly be put in dangerous situations. Yet the more dangerous the situation, whether I'm against an enemy or an adversary, the more I will experience the kind of Christianity that God wants for me.

My protection is seen in the cloud by day and the fire by night. As long as that is over me, it is shielding me from anything the enemy can do. There is my security.

▼

Trust and Obey

But we never can prove
  The delights of His love,
Until all on the altar we lay;
  For the favor He shows,
  And the joy He bestows,
Are for them who will trust and obey.

John H. Sammis (1846–1919)

7

Coming against Our Enemy

*O heavenly Father, may we turn away from the un-
believing world with all its self-confidence, self-reliance,
arrogance, pride, mad pleasures, and ornate love of fine
and rich things. Turn us, we pray Thee, from it all, not
only in our hearts, but in reality, and then turn us to
Jesus Christ, Thy Son. We need Him, Lord; He gave
up His life for the world, and if He had not, we would
be in a vacuum. Take us to Jesus Christ, who is Thy
radiant source of everlasting light and peace and joy
and a world without end. Bless us as we go on—we ask
it in Christ's name, amen.*

Two of the greatest considerations for us as Christians are how we treat our enemies and knowing who our enemies are.

We first have to identify these enemies and realize that they are enemies and not friends.

Exodus 23:27 says, "I will send my fear before thee, and will destroy all the people to whom thou shalt come, and I will make all thine enemies turned their backs unto thee."

This is the blueprint for treating our enemies. Religious persons often try to make the enemy afraid of them on their own. They swell up, look dignified, and, as they say, defend themselves. Their arguments are very long; they write letters and act as if they are insulted. It just never works. The enemy is not intimidated by anything we could ever do or say. He is laughing in our faces.

God says, "I am working for you. I take your place, I accept your enemies as my enemies, and they must deal with me." That should resound a glorious hallelujah in our hearts, because when God steps in, you know something is going to take place. Enemies will have to deal with God. If they had to deal with me, they could overwhelm me with no problem.

It's common to hear people say, "I'm going to have your back." Whether they really do depends on the situation. But when God says, "I have your back," it is an altogether different scenario. God is in it for the long term, eternity. When God acts, He acts based on His knowledge, wisdom, and power. When we act, we act upon our knowledge, wisdom, and power, which, I must say, is quite limited compared with God's, which is unlimited.

One of the great parts of being a Christian is living on the right side, which means that Someone else is in control, and that Someone else is God. When we allow Him to take control, our adversaries must flee. He will make them "turn their backs." No enemy or adversary can stand before us. They cannot stand before God because God stands between them and us and throws a secret, mysterious fear over our enemies, a fear they cannot dismiss or resist.

The cloud by day and fire by night stand between our enemy and us.

This is a wonderful concept for us to consider. When God begins to work, He shrouds the enemy with unexplainable fear. The enemy and adversary do not fear us. We need to understand God is the One who controls all of this, and when they come up against God, they come up against something frightful, something filled with an essence of doom. When God stirs up their fear, He shreds their strength before Him and they turn their backs and run away.

Now a question I want to pose is, How can the adversary be defeated and destroyed in our lives? How can we deal with all of the things that come our way? I think there is one thing we can do and we must do, and let me lay it out before you.

I want you to consider and then accept this covenant that I present to you. Vow never to defend yourself, and then keep that vow for the rest of your life.

We like to defend ourselves. We like to get even. We like to stand up and, as we say, give a testimony and a witness. However, we need to come to a point where we refuse to defend ourselves. We are very limited and can never overcome the enemy. When we permit God to be our protector, the enemy is utterly defeated.

God will defend you.

God, however, will let you protect yourself if that is your choice. God will let you take a stand against the enemy. Many of us have done just that and we know the consequences. However, we must recognize God is on our side and has our back. My enemy and my adversary are now God's enemy and adversary, and He knows how to deal with them.

When we permit God to be our protector, the enemy is utterly defeated.

Vow that you will never defend yourself and will turn every situation over to God. You're afraid, as I am, of being embarrassed and humiliated before the enemy. But if God is on our side, we never have to fear that. Many times my humiliation has been the defeat of the enemy in the long term. I only think of now. God is thinking in terms of eternity. Put your trust in God's ability and strength and wisdom to defend you, to defeat the enemy in your life, and you will see a victory you have never experienced before.

Too often we embrace our enemy as though it were our friend. The enemy has convinced us of this, much to our shame. We fail to read the full story of Israel and how, when they embraced their enemy, they lost.

Embracing the enemy cost Israel quite a bit. And when we do the same, it also costs us. We need to have the discernment to know who our enemy really is. Only the Holy Spirit can reveal these things to us, and as we work with the Holy Spirit, He will begin to give us understanding.

The key ingredient in defeating the enemy is obedience to God. When I vow not to defend myself, I need to obey that vow no matter the difficulties that I encounter. If I think I can handle my situation all by myself, I am facing defeat before I even start.

When I vow not to defend myself, I am saying that I do not have what it takes to come against the enemy. Normally, we do not want to admit this. We like to believe that we can handle every situation.

Just like Israel, I need to remember that God is not trying to glorify me; rather, He wants to glorify himself through my life. This comes only by completely surrendering my heart and life to the Lord Jesus Christ.

I Surrender All

All to Jesus I surrender,
All to Him I freely give;
I will ever love and trust Him,
In His presence daily live.

I surrender all,
I surrender all.
All to Thee, my blessed Savior,
I surrender all.

Judson W. Van DeVenter
(1855–1939)

8

A Prepared Place for a Prepared People

▼

*O Lord, we love Thy church. We love Thy kingdom.
Lord Jesus, we pray for Thy church. We pray for Thy
people who believe Thy Word. We pray that Thou
wouldst revive the church today, revive every denomi-
nation that stands for the Word of God. Save us from
fear and intimidation that come from neglecting the
Holy Spirit. Help us, O God, to keep from quenching
the Holy Spirit. We have listened to those who ought to
know better, and they have made us afraid to believe in
the power of the Holy Ghost. O God, we apologize for
this. Wash us clean and make us white as snow. Lead us,
O Holy Spirit. Help us to walk in the way of truth and
power and purity. And we ask this in Jesus' name, amen.*

We touched on it earlier, but a key phrase in Exodus 23:20 is "to bring thee into the place which I have prepared."

This was the purpose of God for Israel all along. He would bring them into the land to possess what He had promised them. He could not give them their land while they were in a foreign land. In Egypt, they could never experience the blessings of Canaan, the land of the promise.

I firmly believe God's purpose in Christ is the same for us today. He wants to give us, as Christians, a glorious inheritance. As you study the Scriptures you see all of the wonderful promises of God, not only in the Old Testament but also in the New Testament. For those who are followers of Christ, we have what He has promised because of the Lord Jesus Christ.

But He cannot give us our blessed land while we are still in the evil land. While we are still wandering in our own land of Egypt, we can never experience the promises God has for us. This explains the problem with many today. They think they can enjoy the promises of God while still living in the evil land. Such is simply not the case.

One thing we need to comprehend is that God saves us *out of* to bring us *into*. God saved Israel out of Egypt in order to bring them into the promised land.

From my point of view, many gospel Christians today accept the importance of getting people saved out of Egypt.

That is the real focus for them. And it is true—God saves us from our past sins, from our worst habits, and above all else, He is to save us from hell. Coming to Christ means that. And people think, *Now I don't have to worry about those things. I'm not going to hell when I die. I will go zooming off into heaven. Now I can just enjoy life because I know where I'm going when I die.*

God saves us *out of* to bring us *into.*

However, almost nothing is said about what we are saved unto. Yes, we know what we are saved from, and we can glory in that, but that needs to be a temporary glory. We need to know what we have been saved unto.

I want you to know that this is not automatic. Once we are out of Egypt, we do not pitch a tent and say, "Well, I have arrived." No, the truth is effective only when we emphasize that we have been saved not only from something, but we have been saved unto something. Then the description of what we have been saved unto is important for us to be motivated to go in that direction.

Christians will not seek to enter a land of which they have not heard. How can I go somewhere I've never heard about? What is it? How do I get there? The evidence is quite prominent. We have a decaying Christianity, rotten from head to foot, as Bible scholar William Reed Newell wrote in his commentary on Romans.[1] I could not agree more.

So what is this land of promise? What is it that God has set before us? How can we enter in with all of His blessings and receive all of His promises? The things in the land of promise are those chosen for us by God out of the goodness of His heart. This land of promise has been secured by God's oath and covenant. All the infinite resources of God are behind the covenant. What God has promised He can deliver because He is God.

It's not a primitive land awaiting development. This Canaan land was not waiting for Israel to come in, fix it up, and develop it to their own pleasure. No, it was a land already prepared by God for His people, who were fully prepared to inherit it (Deuteronomy 6:10–11; Joshua 24:13).

When we look at this, we need to understand that God could do this in impeccable righteousness. He is the sovereign God of the universe, and everything is His to dispose of as He wills.

Go back to the Old Testament when Israel is leaving Egypt and going toward Canaan. Those nations in Canaan were a moral plague and had forfeited their right to live. And now God is allowing Israel to go into that land where they inherit all of the promises of God based on the character and nature of God himself. They do not create the promised land, they simply enter.

What God has for us is not based on who we are, but rather who He is.

As Christians, we need to remember our spiritual inheritance is a gift from God. God is giving it to us by covenant, by His authority. Out of His sovereign goodwill and good-heartedness, He has opened up the treasures of heaven for us.

What God has for us is not based on who we are, but rather who He is. Because God is good-hearted, we have all of creation, we have the image of God, we have the wondrous personality of God. We have the Bible, we have a Savior, we have the Holy Spirit, we have victory, we have guidance. All of these things are the fruit of the land before us as believers.

God has not left one thing short of His glory. And so as we go into our spiritual inheritance, we do so by the pleasure of God, by the guidance of God, and by the sovereignty and authority of God. We are going to the place God has ordained for us, and we will enjoy the blessings He has established there.

Count Your Blessings

When you look at others with their lands and gold,
Think that Christ has promised you His wealth
    untold;
Count your many blessings, money cannot buy
Your reward in heaven, nor your home on high.

Johnson Oatman, Jr. (1856–1922)

9

Delighting in Our Spiritual Inheritance

▼

O God, our help in ages past, our hope for years to come. We thank Thee, Thou Creator of all creation, and we grieve that we ever marred that creation by sinning. Having done that, we rejoice in that love that saves us, the sacrifice of our Lord. He who was from the beginning hung on a tree that He might die. We can never thank Thee enough. We pray Thee for those who are lost in our midst. O Holy Spirit, may the weary hear the voice of Jesus say, "Come unto me, and rest"; may the thirsty hear Him say, "Come unto me, and drink"; may the blind hear Him say, "Come unto me and see"; may the dead hear Him say, "Come unto me, and live." O Lord, we pray this in Jesus' name, amen.

D o you believe you have everything you could want in life? God is not going to withhold anything from you. Even so, many of us are hindering that inheritance from coming into our lives. Just like Israel, we are wandering in the wilderness, missing our spiritual inheritance in Canaan, the land of plenty.

We can have as much of God as we will take.

This I call the law of appropriation (Joshua 1:1–9). There is no limit with God, and therefore there is no limit to how far we can come into the spiritual inheritance and enjoy all of the great gifts and graces and mercies of God each and every day.

I need to stress this, because as we examine ourselves, we need to know whether we are the kind of Christian we want to be. If we want to draw upon our own strength, God will not forbid it. On the other hand, if we want to access the great mercy and grace of God, we have an open door. We have resources we have not yet tapped into, which is why it is so pathetic to struggle and fight battles that have long been over. Remember, God has put before us the land of promise, and He did not lead us just to let us be dormant or passive. He brought us into that land to enjoy all of the delicacies of His amazing grace.

Christians who slumber and do not progress spiritually are a great affront to the grace of God.

My biggest enemy is not Satan. My worst enemy is myself. If I could let go of the past that God has led me out of and latch on to what God has for me now—the provisions and the access to heaven He has for me—I would begin to experience the kind of Christian life that is full of joy, praise, and honor to God.

God wants to lead us and guide us. He has provided all we need. And as we walk with God, we will access strength and grace, enabling us to rise above our circumstances and our enemy and praise and worship God. God did not save us and lead us out of Egypt so that we could be burdened the rest of our lives. God led us out in order to lead us into a land of milk and honey. A land of rejoicing and praise to enjoy the rest of our lives.

God wants to lead us and guide us. He has provided all we need.

There are people who think they know how to do everything and have their lives under control. But for those of us who have a great desire for God to guide us, this leading is for us. As we tap into God's intention for us, we realize that His Word is our guidance day by day. Just as we are made new every morning, God's mercies are new for us every day. God's purpose is to guide us down the pathway of victory and glory.

All of this is also for the local church—for your church, for my church. It is for those believers who gather together to seek the guidance and direction of God. God wants to take churches out of bondage and bring them into the glorious victory of Canaan land.

The pathway is littered with opposition and enemies and adversaries, but God has said that He would take care of us, lead us, and guide us. Once we surrender ourselves to God and allow His wisdom to be our wisdom, we have nothing more to fear. We can embrace the leadership and guidance of God the Holy Spirit as He leads us in a path that we probably could never imagine ourselves.

I learned this early in my Christian life and ministry. When I was being interviewed for ordination, there were men on the committee who did not think I was qualified. They were right in many regards.

I never finished high school; I went to one day of eighth grade. I never went to college or seminary or any other thing of that nature. I just began preaching on the street corners as I believed God was leading me. I preached in summer tent meetings and on street corners and did all this to the glory of God. I wasn't a very good preacher. I freely admit that. However, I really had a heart to serve God. I later found out that most of the people in that ordination committee were not going to let me be ordained. After they had all talked about it, one man apparently said, "I don't know—I have a feeling about this young man. I think he has a real heart for God and for ministry. I think we should consider ordaining him and just put him in God's hands."

I did not understand it back then, but God was directing me into an area that I did not know anything about. If I had tried to get ordained on my own credentials, I never would have been ordained. God and the Angel of the Lord were leading me in the direction God wanted me to go.

Years later, I can look back and thank God that He was in control of my life. Every decision that I have made I have tried to base on the wisdom of God.

If we let God lead us and give up our own wisdom, He will lead us on a path that we never imagined we would be on.

I am where I am today because of the wisdom of God in opening up the right doors at the right time.

▼

Thy Ways, O Lord, with Wise Design

Thy ways, O Lord, with wise design
Are framed upon Thy throne above,
And every dark and bending line
Meets in the center of Thy love.

Ambrose Serle (1742–1812)

10

Making Our Enemies Work for Us

▼

Father, bless Thou this truth to our hearts. O God, Thy mercies are abundant. Now we pray that Thou wilt help us lean back upon Thy mercy and trust and not be afraid, hate sin, love righteousness, flee from iniquity, and follow after godliness. We know that in all we do, mercy is around us like the earth underneath us, the air above us, and the stars in the heavens. We live in a merciful world and serve a merciful God; we live, move, and have our being in the abundant mercies of the triune God. Graciously grant us, we pray Thee, to understand this and apply it to our hearts in Jesus Christ our Lord, amen.

We need to know God is not sending us—He is leading us. "And when he putteth forth his own sheep, he goeth before them, and the sheep follow him: for they know his voice" (John 10:4).

We must take confidence and comfort in the fact that God is not driving us into some valley somewhere. Rather, like the shepherd who leads his sheep and goes before them, God goes before us and leads us into situations He has already prepared for us.

When we think of Israel, we know God saw all the land and prepared it for them. So we need to recognize that God has seen the land to which He is leading us and has prepared that land for us. We will never be alone because the presence of God will always be with us. Knowing we are not in this battle alone should bring us much comfort and joy.

Much needs to be said about the presence of God. Many Christians, I am sure, have never really experienced this. We talk about it and read about it, but have we really experienced that overwhelming sense of the presence of God? I often think of Jacob when he woke up after that dream of the ladder to heaven, and what he said is always in my mind, "Surely the Lord is in this place; and I knew it not" (Genesis 28:16).

As a Christian, I must remember that God is with me and leading me to a place He has chosen for me. Sometimes I am not aware of His presence, but that does not mean He is not with me. It simply means I need to refocus my heart on the Lord Jesus Christ, regardless of what it takes.

We do not need to figure out our own way. Some Christians make their own plans and design their own Christian life. This is not what God would have for us. The destiny is created and established by God, and so is the pathway. God leads us down His pathway, and He does not necessarily honor our directions. The sooner we reject our plans, the sooner we can delight in the plans God has for us.

The sooner we reject our plans, the sooner we can delight in the plans God has for us.

I know we find this frustrating at times, but God is the one who is in control. If I am where God wants me to be, I will have everything God wants me to have to be all He wants me to be right now. He is never shortsighted. He knows everything. One of His attributes is omniscience.

We do not need to figure out our own road map or how we are going to go or what we are going to do. We need to be careful that we stay in His presence, and this is the work of faith.

I need to cultivate the presence of God in my own life. Regardless of what it takes, I need to make sure I am living in the awe-inspiring mystery of God. The devotional writer Rudolf Otto called this the *mysterium tremendum*.

As Israel went into the promised land, they faced many enemies. These enemies were not there by accident. Rather, these enemies were there by God, and God had prepared Israel to deal with these enemies. We must recognize that Israel did not deal with these enemies on their or the enemy's terms, but rather on God's terms. God was preparing them for their destination.

Their story is just like that of David and Goliath. Remember when David stood up against Goliath? Goliath had all the latest armory for battle at that time. David said, "Thou comest to me with a sword, and with a spear, and with a shield: but I come to thee in the name of the Lord of hosts" (1 Samuel 17:45). Israel never faced their enemy on the enemy's terms. It was always on God's terms.

Remember when Joshua walked around Jericho once a day for six days and then on the seventh day went around seven times? That was not the work of military strategy; it was God at work dealing with the enemy in His way.

Now Israel's enemies were many and sophisticated and had prospered in the land. They had been working for Israel but did not know it. They did not know that what they had would one day belong to the nation of Israel.

And, when Israel left Egypt, they left carrying the wealth of Egypt with them. God always prepares us for the journey.

Now, who were the enemies of Israel?

The Amorites, who inhabited Hebron, Jarmuth, Lachish, and Eglon.

The Perizzites, who were the inhabitants of the valleys.

The Canaanites, who were in Jericho and Ai.

The Hittites, who were at Mount Hermon and Mount Lebanon and in the land of Mizpah.

The Jebusites, who were in the city of Jerusalem.

These were deeply entrenched in the land. They had built their kingdoms from the mountaintops to the valleys to the seas. What they had was valuable, but God decided to dispose them of all their wealth because of their rebellion against God. Read about that in the Old Testament. Their sin brought consequences—God took what they had and gave it to the nation of Israel, His people.

These accounts were written for our instruction. Our worst enemies can become our best helpers. Our spiritual riches may lie in enemy hands. And we must look for them there.

The path is never easy, but God has prepared us for every contingency. His great delight is to give you that which He has prepared for you.

Faith Is the Victory

Encamped along the hills of light,
Ye Christian soldiers, rise.
And press the battle ere the night
Shall veil the glowing skies.
Against the foe in vales below
Let all our strength be hurled.
Faith is the victory, we know,
That overcomes the world.

Faith is the victory! Faith is the victory!
O glorious victory, that overcomes the world.

John Henry Yates (1837–1900)

11

Those Enemies Whose Riches We May Possess

▼

O Lord Jesus, we pray Thy blessings upon us. Thou Lamb of God, we love Thee so we would be like Thee. Only Thy Holy Spirit can cleanse our hearts and bring us into complete and absolute harmony with Thy holy character and nature. We pray that Thou wilt help us to be humbled by our own unworthiness in the knowledge and haunting memories of sins committed. They are many, but they do not in anywise compromise our relationship with Thee. Thy grace is sufficient to release us from those penalties in the past. We love Thee, and we desire to live in a way that will bless Thee. Help us, O Father, to understand Thy Word, and help us to apply it to our daily lives. We pray in Jesus' name, amen.

t's not unusual to see enemies as wholly negative. Yet, when Israel entered Canaan, they inherited the riches of the enemies. No matter what the enemy may be, there is some aspect of it that can bring glory and honor to God. It is the defeat of that enemy that reveals this.

Who are our real enemies? What is it that we face on an almost daily basis?

We know who Israel's enemies were, and we know how God helped them overcome each of those enemies to the glory of God. And we need to remember that Israel went into Canaan land as far as they wanted to go. God's sustaining grace was able to take them farther in, but they refused.

What are the enemies we face today?

The first enemy I would mention is our temper. Temper is a sinful dispositional trait, but we must not think we cannot become saintly. Sometimes temper just rises up and we don't have any control over it. Temper is a sword in the hand of sin, but God disposes of sin, and we gain the riches of that victory. When I see that my temper is against me, I can surrender it to God and He can turn it around according to His ways for me.

Another enemy would be inferiority complexes. That is, it is called by some an inferiority complex. Some people allow the enemy to retain this as a weapon against them. Others exploit it for God's glory. My inferiority just shows me that I cannot do something, but God can do it through me. If I think I can handle my own situation, I'm really going to be in trouble, but when I feel inferior, I can look to God and God can open up to me the riches of His grace.

Sometimes people have to hit rock bottom to realize their strength is compromised in front of this enemy. They think they are bold and walking in strength, but the end result is that they fall on their faces. When I see that my inferiority is my enemy, I have an opportunity to turn it over to God, and God can step in and be my strength at that moment.

Another enemy that we might have is carnal ambition. Remember the New Testament Saul, who later became the apostle Paul? Saul was ambitious to climb the ladder of religion as it was in those days. He was going after Christians like nobody in his day. Then God took that ambition and switched it around, and that ambition that once wanted to destroy the church was now establishing the church across the country and around the world. When Saul became Paul and surrendered that carnal ambition to God, He used it for His mighty work.

When I realize how weak I am, I then can discover how strong my God is.

Another enemy is timidity. We are timid about something and try to cover it up and overcompensate, and this can throw us back on God. When I realize how weak I am, I then can discover how strong my God is, and so my weakness, which can be my enemy, can now be turned around and lead me in the paths of God's graciousness. Knowing what my weakness is enables me to turn that section of my life over to God.

Rebellion is also an enemy of Christians. If you look at the Old Testament, you will find prophets and reformers who were rebellious. That rebellion against God can be switched around and turned against the enemies of God. That which was once my enemy, a rebellion against God, now becomes a weapon for the kingdom of God.

There are other enemies we need to include here.

People, for one, could be our enemy. Their criticism and abuse can actually bring us the riches of humility. When we begin to realize that we are not as big and smart as we think we are, humility enables us to really grasp the riches of God's grace.

Satan, of course, is our enemy. No question about that. His enmity rouses God (Ezekiel 36:2–11).

We understand to a certain degree how Satan is our enemy, but for an example, look at the life of Job. Satan was the enemy of Job, but God used Satan's attack and turned it around to be a blessing to Job. All that Satan did was to clear the way for God to bring into Job's life riches he did not have before. Sometimes God allows Satan to do this kind of thing. He is our enemy, but sometimes Satan clears the way for God to begin a new work, and the thing about it is, Satan does not know that he is actually helping God in His work.

Judas Iscariot, an enemy of Christ, was actually used by God to orchestrate the crucifixion of the Lord Jesus Christ. If it had not been Judas, I am sure there would have been somebody else, but Judas was used of God to bring Jesus to the cross to die for the sins of the world.

When circumstances are against us, God says, "I will be an enemy unto thine enemies" (Exodus 23:22). When we identify our enemy, we realize that we are not facing that enemy alone, but rather God is the enemy to our enemy. The sovereign God can and will oppose every enemy that is before us. When we trust Him and allow Him to do what He wants to do, He can turn all of our enemies against themselves. We experience victory when we receive this great blessing from God.

To know my enemy is the first step, but it is only the first step. Encountering my enemy at first intimidates me and can tempt me to want to quit. But when I see my enemy from God's point of view, my heart is filled with rejoicing because that enemy only reveals to me the amazing grace of God in my life. For He promises, "No weapon that is formed against thee shall prosper; and every tongue that shall rise against thee in judgment thou shalt condemn. This is the heritage of the servants of the Lord, and their righteousness is of me, saith the Lord" (Isaiah 54:17).

Victory through Grace

Conquering now and still to conquer,
    rideth a King in His might;
Leading the host of all the faithful
    into the midst of the fight;
See them with courage advancing,
    clad in their brilliant array,
Shouting the Name of their Leader,
    hear them exultingly say:
Not to the strong is the battle,
    not to the swift is the race,
Yet to the true and the faithful
    vict'ry is promised through grace.

Frances J. Crosby (1820–1915)

12

Out of the Wilderness

▼

Gracious heavenly Father, I pray Thy blessing upon Thy Word today. Help me understand Thy ways and Thy truth. I pray that our faith might mount up like an eagle, stretch its broad wings, and soar so high that nothing can pull it down. The eagle can look upon the sun, and I pray that we may look upon Thy holy Son at the right hand of the Majesty on high. May we be grateful to the point of tears and tenderness that He is God, and very God himself. I praise Thee, O Father, that Thy Son hung on yonder tree for all of our sins and depravity. His blood covers all of that sin; we but need to confess it and repent, and He is faithful to cleanse us from all unrighteousness. Bless us, O Father, as we seek Thee today. I ask this in Jesus' name, amen.

Throughout this book, I am trying to show that God's loving plan for His ransomed ones is twofold.

First, it is to bring them out of the land of bondage, and second, it is to bring them into the land of promise. These two things go together.

It does no good to bring them out if He is not going to bring them into something better. What would be the purpose in that? Still, even though Canaan was the land of plenty, it was also the territory of Israel's enemy. But God knew best. He did not leave Israel's actions to human wisdom or determination. "Thou shalt not bow down to their gods," He told them in Exodus 23:24.

If you would conquer your enemies, you must not imitate them. Your victory lies in being different from them and contrary and even hostile to them. In Exodus 3:17 is a sacred calling into the promised land. Israel was not to allow the inhabitants of the land, along with their gods and idols, to challenge or compromise their relationship with God. They were not to go in and take over the religion and gods of the enemy. Rather, they were to go and destroy the enemy, destroy the gods of the enemy, and bring themselves to a place of worshiping and honoring the God who was leading them there.

They were to go in and overthrow and break down the enemy and their gods. They had their marching orders—not to conform, but rather to contradict.

Many tender-minded Christians today demur here. They want spiritual victory, the land, etc., but they shrink from the iconoclasm. They think of Christianity as gentle and yielding, possibly a consequence of artistic pictures. They see these pictures painted by the great artists of the past and somehow that gives them a notion of what the Christian life is all about.

They do not see Christians as a group that should break down and destroy the enemy. They are too weak to consider the truth that Christ was a revolutionist. He was not crucified for His good works, but He was crucified for being a revolutionist.

All of the apostles died a martyr's death but one. The early church defied the Roman Empire and was punished for it. The cross stands forever as a judgment against the world around us.

Exodus 23:25 says, "Ye shall serve the Lord your God." This is the highest moral imperative. All else depends upon this. All their gods and altars to them must go down. They must be overthrown and broken down under the command and leadership of God, and we must choose to serve Jehovah our God only.

There are other gods and other altars that we need to contend with. We have the god of worldly pleasure. Exodus 32:6 says, "The people sat down to eat and to drink, and rose up to play." This god is worshiped without shame, the god of worldly pleasure. The sad part of it is that it is being brought into the church today. If you cannot entertain them, you cannot attract them.

We also have the god of carnal flesh. In Israel, the manna was despised, and they wanted flesh in their mouth. But God gave them manna for a purpose, and they were not satisfied with what God gave them—they wanted something more.

Then there is the altar of popular religion. Jezebel and Elijah were at each other because Elijah did not represent the popular religion. He stood against everything the world and religion stood for.

We also have the altar of compromise. Daniel and his three young friends—Shadrach, Meshach, and Abednego—and Nehemiah all refused to compromise even though it cost them. God saved them. If you want God to guide you, then God is going to guide you into places where you are not supposed to compromise in any regard.

Then we have the altar of comfort. This is serving God at our convenience. This seems to be the popular attitude today: "Yes, I want to serve God, but only when convenient for me and when I have some spare time."

Amos 6:1 says they were "at ease in Zion." How can you be at ease when you have an enemy in front of you? Jesus said in Luke 9:23, "If any man will come after me, let him deny himself, and take up his cross daily, and follow me." How can we be followers of Jesus and insist on convenience and comfort?

We also have the god of intimidation. This is ruling by fear, warnings, and threats. Whatever intimidates the other person, this is the god that brings it about. Intimidation is the tool of religion to get the people in order.

We also have the god of mammon. The only time Jesus used the whip was when the people were selling things in the temple that should not have been sold. They were trying to make a profit. Then they were giving after they made their profit despite the fact that what they were doing was contrary to temple rules. If it is done for a good cause, it must be okay.

Then we have the altar of culture. Christianity, I am afraid, has become cultural, elevating, and refining. But the culture of the world is treacherous and in no way honors the cause or calling of Christ. Jesus was a revolutionary against His culture, and the church today has to follow in His train.

> The culture of the world is treacherous and in no way honors the cause or calling of Christ.

The Scripture tells us, "He shall bless thy bread, and thy water; and I will take sickness away from the midst of thee" (Exodus 23:25). God fulfilled this while Israel obeyed. And He'll do the same for us. If we obey Him, He will allow the blessings to come upon our heads, but we cannot serve God and mammon. Obedience is making the choice. We cannot have it both ways. There is a point in our Christian experience where we need to obey Christ, choose His way, and go against the way of the world.

▼

Trust and Obey

When we walk with the Lord in the light of His Word,
  What a glory He sheds on our way!
While we do His good will, He abides with us still,
  And with all who will trust and obey.
Trust and obey, for there's no other way
  To be happy in Jesus, but to trust and obey.

John H. Sammis (1846–1919)

13

Finding God's Will Means Serving and Trusting

▼

Heavenly Father, lift my eyes to Thee, to Thy Son, Jesus Christ the Lord, who is above angels. Thou sittest at the right hand, and I pray, give to me a spiritual urgency, a longing that is more than human. Give to me the desire that is like a fire burning in my bones. O God, may I not be content with where I am and in what I am. But I pray that Thou wouldst stir up my heart with the longing and desire for Thee that can only be experienced in Thy presence. Lift up my heart unto Thee I ask, O Father, in Jesus' name, amen.

cannot repeat it enough: God is bringing out His people for the purpose of bringing them into a land He has prepared for them. Israel was not going into a land flattened and deserted, but a land already prepared.

To do this, God led them to a place He chose, but not a place the people themselves chose. God established the destination. He chose the way they were to go. It may not look great from our point of view, but when God prepares the way, our responsibility is to trust and follow, come what may. They did not determine how to go in, they only determined that they would follow God, and consequently He opened up the way for them.

Exodus 23:25 says, "Ye shall serve the Lord your God." Understanding what this means will serve us very well. If I am going to progress in my Christian experience, I need to understand what it really means to serve God.

Now, the word *serve* may have twenty-six meanings in the English dictionary, but we can make it mean anything, I suppose. In the Hebrew, it means to work for a master as a bondservant. It is important for us to keep in mind that serving means we are not directing or dictating, but rather, we are submitting to a master.

Jacob worked for Rachel's hand in marriage for what he thought would be seven years, but it turned out to be fourteen. Israel worked for the Egyptians for 400 years before God led them out. Serving God is important to my relationship with Him.

As I learn how to serve and submit myself to His authority, I begin to go in the direction He wants me to go.

The problem with many Christians today is that they want to tell God how they are going to serve, as well as the conditions of their serving. This is not acceptable as far as God is concerned. God is my owner, and serving Him means I recognize His ownership and I am completely in allegiance to Him, nobody else. To obey, to trust, to love, to worship—these are the elements that enrich our acts of serving God.

If we are going to serve God, it is imperative that we learn what obedience to God is all about. Many people want God's gifts, but they do not want to obey Him. In the meantime, they want God to give them what they want, when they want it. Obedience is a primary ingredient of my service to God. A missing characteristic of Christian religion today is the knowledge that to obey is better than sacrifice. No matter what comes my way, obedience to God is the thing that is really important.

I need to really think about this to see if I'm willing to obey God at all costs. Am I willing to turn my back on all other things in order to obey God? That is a question that needs to be pondered carefully and prayed over in a way that we will come to loyalty to God and God alone.

Another key element in our service has to be trust. God demands that we trust Him completely. This is where we get into trouble because we think trust is based on knowing everything about a situation. But that's not the case. God wants us to trust Him even though we have no idea what our next step is. If I can't trust God, whom then can I trust? Religious leaders? Government leaders? Whom am I going to trust if I cannot really trust God?

Another question might be, Who has my best interest in mind? Is it the religious leaders, government leaders, or anyone else? Or is it God? Does God have my best interest in mind as He brings me into a situation of serving Him and trusting Him for the next steps along the way?

Am I willing to turn my back on all other things in order to obey God?

Part of this trust has to be confidence in a Person. Do I have confidence in God that He is leading me down the right path, no matter what I may see along the way? I think confidence is a part of friendship. My friendship with God has brought me to a place where I have confidence in Him, and that confidence is expressed in trusting Him with everything He sends my way.

Another element quite important is love. The Bible teaches us that God is love and all of love. When we think of love, we need to think of God.

I know when we think of love today, many times we are thinking of celebrities in Hollywood and the world's evaluation of love. We need to quickly move away from that and really center on God's love. What do I understand about God's love that will enable me to serve Him in a way that will honor and please Him?

I think this love is based on an increasing intimacy with God, which leads to an intensified love. My love of God is going to lead me to trust Him no matter the situation.

The last one would be worship. No matter what is in our pathway, no matter how and in what direction God is leading us, we are to let the whole thing go into His hands and fall before Him in trembling adoration.

Does this generation of Christians know how to participate in a real spirit of adoration? Do we know what God is doing in our lives in such a way that we can trust Him enough to adore and worship Him above all other things?

The world has their gods they worship so vehemently. As a believer in Christ, I want my worship of God to be the strongest aspect of my life. I want everything in my life to flow out of my adoring wonder and worship of the Lord Jesus Christ.

Many people seek guidance selfishly. They want to know what they can get out of a situation. They do not serve the Lord our God, but they serve individuals, they serve the church, and they serve all kinds of things, but they never really push aside everything and serve God. You see, when I am serving God, I am in the proper place of fellowship with other believers. If I am serving a church instead of God, then I compromise much of my fellowship with other believers. Illustrations of this are too numerous to even begin to list.

We can have His presence, the Angel before us, if we will meet His conditions. And that's the important thing. I cannot try to figure out my pathway. I simply need to serve Him, and in serving Him, I am completely coming under His conditions. Does not Jesus say, "My yoke is easy, and my burden is light" (Matthew 11:30)? His commandments are not grievous. When I get to know God, I begin to see that He has my best interest in mind for the longest period of time.

O Master, When Thou Callest

O Master, when Thou callest,
　　No voice may say Thee nay,
For blest are they that follow
　　Where Thou dost lead the way;
In freshest prime of morning,
　　Or fullest glow of noon,
The note of heavenly warning
　　Can never come too soon.

　　　　　　Sarah G. Stock (1839–1898)

14

With His Direction Comes His Provision

▼

O Father, I pray in the name of the Lord Jesus Christ
for help. I know that the world, the flesh, and the devil
conspire to grab away every seed that is sown, every
holy impulse, every high intention, and every sacred
vow. Undo the work of the devil. Work now in my
heart by cleansing, purifying, sanctifying, delivering,
and setting me free. O great God, I need help by the
heavens. Brains cannot do it. Personality cannot do
it. Training cannot do it. Learning cannot do it. It is
only Thee who can break the power of sin and set the
prisoner free. Only Thou canst open blind eyes, and
only Thou canst move the will to obedience.

We need to keep in mind that there are benefits to serving God. We serve Him because we should. There is no merit in this, no reward due us. It is only right that we should serve Him, and we sin if we do not. We must commit ourselves to serving God in a way that pleases Him and in a way that is not too convenient for us. When we try to serve God based on our convenience, we are in the beginning stage of rebellion against the will of God.

Therefore, anything He gives is by His grace. We are delivered from the bondage of sin and God pours into our lives that which we need. Sometimes God does things in my life that I do not understand at the moment. Down the road a few weeks, a few months, a few years, I begin to see what God was doing and why God did a certain thing in my life. God guided and protected Israel as they went into the land of promise because they committed themselves to serve Jehovah and Him only.

God is so infinite and good with wonderful benefits and blessings far beyond our most optimistic hopes. God enjoys blessing us; His only problem is to get us to believe Him. When we are committed to Him and serve Him, God wants us to really believe what He says He is doing, trust Him, and let Him do it.

There are benefits that we cannot earn.

Exodus 23:25 says, "He shall bless thy bread, and thy water." God will bless our daily bread, what we eat, and will make it what we need at that time.

This will be according to our faith. My life today is what it is because of my faith in God. The more my faith in God develops, the more my life begins to mature in the direction God wants it to go.

Some only see this as spiritual; others rise to claim it for their practical lives. My faith in God certainly has a spiritual aspect, but there are also practical aspects. I need to trust God and have faith as I go down the pathway where He is leading. He does not send me unequipped; He prepares me for the work He has for me to do, and my faith enables me to receive that in His holy name. Frustration comes when I try to do what God has not prepared me to do. In finding God's direction for my life, I will also discover God's provision.

God says, "I will take sickness away" (Exodus 23:25). Our health is ours as we claim it in faith. God has physical blessings for us, and we can trust Him for those as well.

In finding God's direction for my life, I will also discover God's provision.

Patrick, a member of our church long ago, was seated in the balcony at a church meeting. When the invitation was given to come to the altar, Patrick ran all the way down to the altar and fell on his knees.

Somebody later asked, "Patrick, why did you run to the altar?" He said, "When I heard the invitation given, I knew there was something wrong here that I ought to go down and get straightened out. I heard a voice say, 'Patrick, go down to that altar.' Another voice said, 'Patrick, don't go.' I recognized that second voice. I knew it was the devil. I not only wanted to go, but I ran. I got down there in a hurry to show the devil I was going to go to that altar."

Patrick was a chef in one of the finest hotels in this country. He and his wife had a son in his twenties, Lawrence, who was born unable to walk. Patrick believed the Lord would heal him, but He did not. One day he said to God, "I am not going to eat again until my boy is healed." His wife said, "Do you think that's wise, Patrick?" He said, "Leave that to God and me."

So Patrick went to work, and the first day was not so bad, but the second and third days were terrible. In this fine, high-class restaurant, he was dishing up food that was just utterly out of this world for these high-class patrons. Still, Patrick remained steadfast. He told his wife, "Until Lawrence is healed, I am fasting. I am leaning on God."

One morning he heard his wife's scream that filled the room. He ran into the room and said, "What's the matter?" And she said, "Look! Look!" Lawrence was running around all over the room, perfectly delivered.

I would not say that everybody should do that. I would not go that far, and I could not go along with some of the healing evangelists. I will only say, God did that for a simplehearted man who no one else could help.

God says, "The number of thy days I will fulfill" (Exodus 23:26). In the will of God, there is no failure. There are battles along the way, things we must endure along with trials and tribulations. All you have to do is look in the Old Testament and see Joseph and Job and all these men of God who were serving God and trusting God. On their pathway to serving God in the promised land there were many battles, but their faith in God enabled them to succeed and get to the place God wanted them to be.

There is no premature death in the will of God. A man will live as long as God has work for him to do and as long as that man is really committed to that work. When my work is done and I have completed it as God wants me to, then my life is over.

There are no tragedies. Everything that comes into my life comes in such a way that God can mold me and prepare me for the next step. Sometimes a person goes through a terrible misfortune, and as a result of that they go in a direction God wants them to go and they have the faith to trust God. I may not understand why I am going through such a terrible time. The biggest problem I have is not understanding what my problem really is. But I am not to focus on my problems but rather on the Solver of them.

The devil would like to direct my attention away from where God is leading me. He is very successful in doing this, and we need to stand up against the enemy in God's strength, not ours.

The great tragedy is that God will set a time for early promotion if we resist His will. Imagine dying without fulfilling the will of God.

▼

What a Friend We Have in Jesus

Have we trials and temptations?
Is there trouble anywhere?
We should never be discouraged—
Take it to the Lord in prayer.
Can we find a friend so faithful,
Who will all our sorrows share?
Jesus knows our every weakness;
Take it to the Lord in prayer.

Joseph M. Scriven (1819–1886)

15

Blessings and Battles

O heavenly Father, in the precious name of Jesus, I come before Thee opening up my heart for that which Thou hast for me. Thou knowest my way, and I trust Thee day by day to guide me and strengthen me in the way that Thou wants me to go. Father, help me to be an inspiration to those around me that they might not see me, but rather that they might see the Lord Jesus Christ. Fill me, O Father, with Thy glory. Fill me with the grace that is amazing to those who look at it. Lead me in the path that Thou hast for me and make my heart obedient to Thee in all things. I pray this in Jesus' name, amen.

n examining the subject of the cloud by day and the fire by night, I see things that apply to my life today. The Old Testament is the foundation of the theology in the New Testament and our theology today. Knowing how God led Israel is the basis of understanding how He is leading us today.

With that in mind, I believe I am seeing a new interest in the deeper Christian life message. There is a curiosity about a life deeper than the norm. People see the Christian life, but they want to see something deeper and stronger.

We Christians need to cultivate this passion for the deeper life. This is what God has for us. As we see Israel leaving Egypt and going to the promised land under the direction of God, we see the deeper life illustrated for us. I think we need to understand that the theology of the Old Testament carries into the New Testament and still applies to us today.

It is important to stress this deeper life among believers. Too often Christians believe that all they need to do is accept Jesus Christ as their Savior and then everything will be all right. The Christian life must progress deeper and deeper into the things of God, the very heart of God himself.

This message is missing for the most part today. Too many people view Christianity as an insurance policy so that when they die they can go to heaven. They do not see it as a road map leading them into the heart of God. Apart from a personal experience with God and basking in His presence, Christianity does not mean anything. It is just another religion.

As we see Israel in Exodus 23, they are out of Egypt, but not yet in Canaan, the promised land, "the place which I have prepared" (v. 20).

The Christian life must progress deeper and deeper into the things of God.

I think the majority of Christians are in that position today. They are in the desert wandering aimlessly, and before them is the promised land with all of the blessings and glory of God waiting for them. They see it, but they cannot quite understand it or reach it.

It is at this time that the spies from Israel, under the direction of Moses, are sent to spy out the land (Numbers 13:2, 17–25). The spies go into the land and see for themselves what God had in store for them.

This was all with God's approval. God, I believe, is a great realist. He wanted Israel to know what they were facing as they went into Canaan land. He did not want them to be surprised by things they did not consider. Therefore, He had twelve men go ahead, spy out the land, and report back to Israel.

Christ uses this method constantly. For example, He said in John 14:29, "And now I have told you before it come to pass, that, when it is come to pass, ye might believe."

God does not want us to be surprised by what is before us. Surely, there are many things we do not quite understand, and that is where our faith kicks in. He clearly lays out the land before us, if only we would give Him attention as seekers of His Word. All of this is embedded in the Word of God. God wants us to understand that although the promised land is filled with blessings, it is also filled with trials and battles.

All some Christians see are the blessings. Others, all they see are the battles. This is because we are divided and need to come together to see that the blessings and the battles are part of what God has for us.

Now the problem today is romanticism, and it is out of control not only in our culture, but in our churches as well. We have romanticized what it means to be a Christian. And we overemphasize the advantages of Canaan and ignore the enemies. It is particularly true in the evangelical church. We access the positive and forget about the negative. We tell people that the Christian life is peaceful and easy to live. Whereas, the reality is once we enter into Canaan there are battles aplenty. The enemy is trying to keep us from possessing the land that God has for us. Our enemies truly are our enemies, and we should have no affiliation with them.

The spies returned (Numbers 13:25–33). Two of them saw God open the land for their possession (Numbers 14:6–10). The other ten saw the giants in the land, which was all they saw. The majority ruled, which moved them out of God's provision. Those ten spies compromised God's desire for the whole nation of Israel.

This is true today. We emphasize the positive, not allowing people to really understand what is in front of them. We go by majority rule instead of by the Word of God. Some people have the idea that Christianity is a democracy. Rather, it is a theocracy where God's Word is all that matters. If I am obedient to God's Word, then I am on the path He has prepared for me.

As a consequence of majority rule, Israel turned away from the promised land God had for them. Keep in mind that they turned back with God's promises in their ears, with the Angel before them, and with the divinely chosen land waiting for them. In turning back, they turned their backs on God's promise to them. Why is it so many Christians even today turn back when they see the least bit of annoyance or tribulation? Remember what James says, "My brethren, count it all joy when ye fall into divers temptations" (James 1:2). We forget that our rejoicing is in the land of promise. And in the land of promise we will experience trials and tribulations, but in those are found the joy, privilege, and glory of God.

This was a bold decision on the part of Israel. An act of the will led them out of the promised land; at that point, they might have gone in and experienced everything God had for them. However, they turned their backs on God's promise.

The reason people today do not experience all that God has for them is they refuse to go forward into the promised land. The majority vote has won over the will of God, and people are backing away from what God has for them.

We see the results in Numbers 32:7–13. Because of their turning away from where God wanted them to go, Israel experienced the anger of God on them. God's anger burned against Israel, making them travel in the desert for forty years until all the people who had sinned in the eyes of the Lord were destroyed. For forty years, they had to deal with their disobedience.

The deeper Christian life goes forward as God directs and leads us, and we depend upon God to deal with our enemies. God's promise was that He would make Israel's enemies His enemies and their adversaries His adversaries. Israel had nothing to lose in obeying God and everything to lose in disobeying Him.

Deeper and Deeper

Into the heart of Jesus
    Deeper and deeper I go,
Seeking to know the reason
    Why He should love me so,
Why He should stoop to lift me
    Up from the miry clay,
Saving my soul, making me whole,
    Though I had wandered away.

Oswald J. Smith (1889–1986)

16

Our Assurance Is in the Forward Position

▼

Heavenly Father, thank Thee so much for all of Thy promises. As I look at them and meditate upon them day by day, I see Thy nature revealed in these promises. O Father, let me go forward in the power of Thy Holy Spirit and let me access those promises that Thou hast for me. Do not let me turn aside. I trust Thee to give me the grace and the faith to go forward for Thee. Keep me, O Holy Spirit, facing forward and not backward. My past is behind me, and only Thy grace can help me get over my past. But Thine assurance for me is going forward in the power and demonstration of the Holy Spirit. I pray this, O Father, in the name of the Lord Jesus Christ, amen.

need to lay out here the truth that God desires us to go forward. And in order for us to go forward, we must grasp His promises.

Many people look at the promises of God as just something to read and think about and talk about but not to be taken very seriously. However, every promise of God unfolds to us the character and nature of God. As I access these promises, I begin to understand God more than I did before. The more I understand God, the more focused I am on going forward not backward.

When we look at Israel backing away from the promised land, we need to know that their experience applies to us today. We have heard the call, the promise and assurance from God to go forward into the promised land. But some object and oppose it and give an evil report that is a result of fear and prejudice, not really knowing God on a personal level.

Ten of the spies who went into the land brought back a negative report. Two spies brought back a positive report and encouraged the people to go forward. Nevertheless, the majority ruled. We see majority ruling today, backing away from the promises of God.

I am afraid this describes many evangelical churches today. They are so afraid of being called fanatics that they have compromised their forward walk with the Lord. The deeper life is before them with all of its rich blessings, but they are so concerned that people might think of them as fanatical and therefore oppose them. We have the idea today that we need to relate to the culture if we are going to reach people for Christ.

We need to have men and women so committed to Jesus Christ that no obstacle can obscure the presence of God from them. It is the cloud by day and the fire by night that give direction and encourage us to go forward.

The rich life in Christ contradicts the culture around us in just about every aspect. When we see the deeper life, our Canaan, and when we back away from it because the majority is ruling, we lose the promises and blessings God has given to us.

Later on in Israel we find Joshua and Caleb leading a new generation to take the promised land, defeating the enemies, and receiving that which God had for them.

It takes a battle. If you look back through history and see the revivals and reformations that have taken place and all the work of the Holy Spirit, you will see that when a church gets comfortable, it loses a sense of what God has for them.

But we do not want to be uncomfortable. We want to be comfortable, and we want people who come into our churches to be comfortable. We slap them on the back and say, "We're buddies here."

What Joshua and Caleb did is what is needed today. We need a new Joshua and Caleb to lead us forward regardless of the battles that we find along the way. This kind of truth has consequences, and too often, like Israel, we stand at Canaan preferring the wilderness and desert and miss the wonderful promises God has for us.

Not to go forward is to miss what God has for us. Now, when God sets the path, no matter the difficulties that seem to be in the way, God has prepared us for it. No obstacle surprises God; He knows what is ahead and knows how to prepare us, and we need to go forward in His power and trust His wisdom. Many times we try to do it in our own strength and power, but it never works that way.

We need to go forward in the power and demonstration of the Holy Spirit and possess everything God has planned for us. That generation that died in the wilderness—I believe when they saw what God had for them, they were greatly disappointed, and I think we need to step back a little and meditate on the promises of God and see the kind of God we have and what He has promised for us. God is always as good as His promises.

This deeper life is experiencing the promises of God in practical, everyday living.

The promises sometimes are physical, spiritual, and even financial. I believe that God has promised me things that will make my life a blessing not only to me, but also to those around me. Now the problem is that I need to go into the promised land, and I am going to encounter battles and trials that try to stop me. But in going forward in the name of the Lord as David did before with Goliath, I find a power and strength I did not know I had.

It is not just optimism or positive thinking. Rather, it is getting deeper into the things of God. It is getting deeper into the character and nature of God. We then begin experiencing God in a way we have never experienced before. We get out of the desert and into the promised land and begin to enjoy all of the fruit promised by God.

113

Out in the desert they could not enjoy the fruit. They had to have the manna that came every morning, except the Sabbath, and then occasionally God sent quail. Can you imagine eating the same thing day after day after day? I am sure they got tired of it, but it was their fault. They were reaping exactly what they sowed.

Before we can have a victory, we have to have a battle.

Many people today go through the same routine over and over and over again, and they are disappointed with their Christian experience. That is because they are in the desert, and once they get into Canaan, they will nourish their soul on the fruit of the land. They will rejoice in the victories in Canaan. We must keep in mind that before we can have a victory, we have to have a battle. And when that battle is over, we begin to enjoy the promises God has for us.

Getting into the deeper life is a real trial, just like the children of Israel discovered. They left the desert, went into Canaan, and experienced battle after battle. But every battle made them stronger. Every battle prepared them for the next battle. And God was on their side, leading them, and they were walking by the cloud by day and the fire by night, and nobody could resist them.

Coming into this Canaan experience is for every Christian who wants to know God better.

The God of Abraham Praise

The heavenly land I see,
    with peace and plenty blest;
a land of sacred liberty,
    and endless rest.
There milk and honey flow,
    and oil and wine abound,
and trees of life forever grow
    with mercy crowned.

    Attributed to Daniel ben Judah
    (circa 1400) and paraphrased by
    Thomas Olivers (1725–1799)

17

God's Faithfulness to His Word

▼

Heavenly Father, to Thee I look in all reverence. It amazes me that Thou desirest my worship. My delight in worship encourages me to worship Thee all the more. Help me understand how faithful Thou art to Thy Word. Help me, O Father, to realize that in Thy Word I discover the blessings Thou hast for me. I do not deserve anything, and one thing I do thank Thee for is that Thou dost not give me what I deserve. Thou givest me grace and mercy beyond my ability to obtain. Thy faithfulness motivates me to obey Thee in all situations. Praise Thy name, through Jesus Christ my Lord, amen.

Our instructions regarding the Angel before us are to watch with complete attention and reverence. I believe that to be the key element of all of this. Reverence is the door that opens to obeying God. If I do not obey God, I will not go where God wants me to go or when He wants me to go.

The fulfillment of God's promise to Israel was, "Behold, I send an Angel before thee, to keep thee in the way, and to bring thee into the place which I have prepared" (Exodus 23:20).

They saw God's faithfulness when they obeyed and kept their lives reverent before Him. One lacking element in the church today is this sense of reverence. We have frivolity and casualness that have come from the world, and they are dimming our ability to worship God as He deserves. We need to cultivate a spirit of reverence because it is in our reverence that we begin to approach the very presence of God.

Imagine Israel living under the cloud by day and the fire by night. What could be more awesome than knowing and experiencing the amazing presence of God? If I wanted to be a Christian for anything, it would be experiencing the presence of God in my daily life.

If we are to understand the ways of God with man, we need to believe, accept, and receive the benefits now for ourselves and for the church at large. God is working, God is moving, God is leading, and He wants us to receive the benefits of all this work before us. These benefits are not something we have earned; rather, they are something we received from God through our obedience to Him. It is not something that God has to give us because we work for it. It is something God desires to give us because He deserves to give it.

"After the death of Moses . . . the Lord spake unto Joshua" (Joshua 1:1). Israel could have been in the land forty years before, but they failed to take God at His word and simply obey. Their years of wandering around in the desert were their fault and theirs alone. We sometimes fail to realize that most of our problems are self-induced. God is leading us in one direction and we are zigzagging all over the place, going into all kinds of difficulties and problems of our own making. That's not God's plan. God's plan is to lead us into the land in victorious glory.

Their years of wandering were because they had alienated God; His covenant, His purpose, and His promise stood, and they failed to live up to God's promise. Had they not alienated God, His promise would have stood.

Israel now must be detached from Moses. That is the key here. This must have been a great shock for Israel at that time. A whole generation had known only Moses. He had symbolized God's leadership among them. He spoke for God. He was their connection with God and Canaan. God spoke to them clearly and encouragingly and said that they had Him, the Angel before them, the fiery pillar. They didn't need Moses. I think that was hard for them to understand. Moses had been the epitome of their faithfulness to God.

You do not lose God when you lose a man of God. That was something Israel was to learn. Though Moses was gone, that did not mean God had abandoned them.

God is the God of today and tomorrow as well as yesterday. However, to most Christians, God is the God of yesterday alone. They believe in everything that was but cannot rise to believe for today, let alone tomorrow. This was what God was trying to teach Israel at this time.

It is also what God is trying to teach us today. Too many times we look backward and try to relive yesterday when God's plan is in front of us and ahead of us. God desires to lead us into a land of promise, a land of blessing, and a land of fruit.

As we give ourselves to the Lord and trust Him through the bad times, we finally come to see that what God was doing was something we never imagined.

A few years ago when I was in Harrisburg in our office for Christian publications, I was going through some letters in the office, and I ran across a letter dated a long time ago. It was from one of the officers at the top of the Christian and Missionary Alliance. I began to read the letter and it was a bit angry. The letter said something like, "Who is this Tozer, pastor of some church in Chicago, who thinks he can write the biography of A. B. Simpson?"

I had to chuckle to myself because I remembered writing that biography of A. B. Simpson. I remembered it was a real blessing to write it, but here was a man who did not think I was capable of writing it. He was looking from a human standpoint and seeing that this insignificant pastor at some little church in Chicago did not have the means to write a biography of a man as great as A. B. Simpson.

Isn't that always the way God works? When I read that letter I realized that he was absolutely right. There was no way I had within me the talent or ability to write a biography about a man as great as A. B. Simpson. You see, when God led me to write that biography, He empowered me to write it.

When God leads us to do something for Him, He always empowers us to do it. And this is where obedience comes from. I can only obey God when I know what He wants me to do. I may not understand all of the implications of what He wants me to do at the time, but I understand that He wants me to do something, and if He wants me to do something, He will give me the power and ability to do that something.

When God leads us to do something for Him, He always empowers us to do it.

I think we all need to be doing things above our personal, human ability. We need to rise above it and begin living in the power of the Holy Spirit. We need to be doing work not that we are capable of doing, but work that can only come through the power of the Holy Spirit in our lives.

▼

Praise God from Whom All Blessings Flow

Praise God, from whom all blessings flow;
Praise Him, all creatures here below;
Praise Him above, ye heav'nly host;
Praise Father, Son, and Holy Ghost!

Praise God the Father who's the source;
Praise God the Son who is the course;
Praise God the Spirit who's the flow;
Praise God, our portion here below!

Thomas Ken (1637–1711)

18

Canaan Was a Gift from God

▼

Heavenly Father, I praise Thee for the wonderful ways in which Thou blessest me. I cannot count my blessings—they are too many. I try to think of all of the ways Thou hast blessed me, and when I do my heart fills up with such adoration for Thee. And the thing that blesses my heart, O Father, is the fact that my worship is acceptable in Thy presence. Thank Thee, Father, for all Thou hast done. Thank Thee for the blessings Thou hast brought into my life. And I trust that I may continue to worship and praise Thee the rest of my life. Whatever tomorrow holds, I know Thou art holding me. I pray this, O Father, in Jesus' name, amen.

srael left a better place, Egypt, for a worse place, the desert. Almost always, God will let us experience consequences when we stubbornly disobey. Had Israel obeyed God when they left Egypt and entered Canaan, they would have had two things.

First, Moses would have been their leader into Canaan. Second, they would have been in the land of promise enjoying the blessings God had for them.

I cannot overemphasize this—what we seek is a gift to be received, not a reward to be earned. I am not working for my salvation, but I am accepting from God the blessing of being saved by the blood of the Lord Jesus Christ.

I need to understand what God is doing and that He is giving me a gift—I cannot earn anything. Remember what God said: "For every beast of the forest is mine, and the cattle upon a thousand hills" (Psalm 50:10). What could we give to God that He does not already have?

God's blessings are always God's response to our obedience. When Israel refused to go into Canaan, Canaan did not disappear. It was there forty years later when they finally decided to obey God and go in. Even after their long years of blundering in the wilderness, God's gift to them was still available for them, but only on His terms. The trend of faith needed to be resumed so they could go forward and receive that which God had for them. It is as much for us today as it was for them then.

How often do we refuse to go into God's blessing because it looks too difficult for us? How often do we hold back, turn away, and go in the opposite direction when God has put a blessing in front of us? We do not see the blessing—rather, we see the battle.

We do not negotiate with God for these blessings. What leverage would we have against God? The only way we can receive God's blessing is to surrender ourselves completely to Him in unqualified obedience.

When God sets something before us, we should not look at the physical aspect. That is exactly what Israel did. The ten spies only saw the giants, while the two spies saw the glory of God.

When I look at the situation in front of me, I only see the giants, and because of that, I turn away because I know I cannot handle that situation. It is interesting that God puts before us situations that we cannot handle in our own strength so that we can experience and understand the mighty grace and power of our God. It is not impressive when we try to handle the situation, but it is when God enables and empowers us to handle it. It all belongs to God anyway.

I think all believers make the mistake of delaying obedience to God. God had to wait for a whole generation of Israelites to die before He could bring them into the promised land.

Everyone has as much of God and His blessings as he or she wants to have. I have said this before, and I continue to say it: I am today what I am because of my response to God. If I surrender to God, I turn it all over to Him. If I try to make it on my own, I put all that responsibility on myself. The time I am losing and the pain I'm experiencing are the result of disobedience in my heart and not doing things God's way. Everybody is as holy as he or she wants to be. Everybody is as full of the Holy Spirit as he or she wants to be. My desire is to have everything God wants me to have. I know I am going to go through trials and trouble to get there, but getting there is well worth it.

> *Everyone has as much of God and His blessings as he or she wants to have.*

God does not arbitrarily bless us; rather He leads us to His place of blessing. The key is listening to God's voice and obeying. The destination is not of our definition but God's. Everything looks different from our point of view.

For example, when we think of the cloud by day and the fire by night, we are thinking of opposites. During the day, the cloud contradicts the light, and at night the fire contradicts the dark. I find it is difficult to get a handle on that. My circumstances do not define me, but rather, God's work in me always contradicts them.

My joy is not in my circumstance but in that Angel that is before me.

We are the ones opening our hearts to receive as much of God as we will. God does not determine how much we shall have; we decide how much we are going to accept from God. I have prayed and labored unselfishly, and I believe the Holy Spirit has spoken to my heart. I need to put away selfish ambitions, and I need to set before me the Canaan God has for me. When I see what God has for me, and when I begin to see not through my eyes, but through the eyes of the Lord, I will see something worth sacrificing for.

Sacrifice is not a very popular subject these days. But obedience involves some level of sacrifice. The greater the obedience, the greater the sacrifice. And the greater the sacrifice, the greater the gift God has for us. I need to realize that in my own strength I cannot get where God wants me to be. However, God is going to lead me. There is a cloud by day and a fire by night that are going to get me through to the place where God wants me to be.

▼

Channels Only

How I praise Thee, precious Savior,
　　That Thy love laid hold of me;
Thou hast saved and cleansed and filled me,
　　That I might Thy channel be.

Channels only, blessed Master,
　　But with all Thy wondrous grace,
Flowing through us, Thou canst use us
　　Every hour in every place.

Mary E. Maxwell (dates unknown)

19

The Curse of Delayed Blessings

▼

O heavenly Father, I praise Thee today for all the blessings that Thou art pouring upon my life. I confess and apologize for my disobedience and for pushing aside the blessings for something lesser. O God, wean me away from the world, the flesh, and the devil, and allow me to embrace the blessings Thou hast for me. May I put aside all inconveniences and all of the things distracting me, and now may my heart be fixed upon Thee. May I see Thee in front of me in such a way that I can see nothing else. Let me never be discouraged by any delay in the blessings Thou hast intended for me. Help me to be patient and wait upon Thy timing and allow Thee to do what Thou intend to do in my life and through my life. And I pray this, O Father, in Jesus' name, amen.

srael is now standing at the river's edge. Moses is gone. Behind Israel are forty years of unnecessary wandering in the desert wilderness. Again, I emphasize that this wandering was unnecessary. God had prepared them and had prepared the land before them, and they chose to turn their backs on God.

A new generation has come that has no idea what is about to happen, and before them is the blessed land. A land they could have been enjoying for the last forty years. In Joshua chapter 1, we see that Joshua is sent to lead them across the river. Someone must lead and exhort the rest of the people, and it becomes Joshua's responsibility to take them into the land. However, as we know, Joshua is not on his own. We're not, either. As it was so many years ago, the Angel before us will lead us to the land of promise.

If you remember, Joshua and Caleb were the two spies who encouraged Israel to go into the promised land. These two were the ones who saw the giants but looked beyond them and saw the great blessing that God had for Israel. They did not consider what they could do in their own strength, but looked at the land as something that God had for them.

When Caleb came back from spying out the land, he tried to encourage all of Israel to go forward and claim God's promise: "And Caleb stilled the people before Moses, and said, Let us go up at once, and possess it; for we are well able to overcome it" (Numbers 13:30). Caleb understood that their strength to possess the land was God, who was with them.

God never forgot Caleb's trust in God's promises. In God's graciousness He allowed Joshua and Caleb to be the last survivors of that generation that refused to take God at His word. They were the only ones of that generation who experienced the blessings God had promised. He and Joshua knew that God was on their side and that they were not going forward alone.

An unflattering side of human nature is that one rarely finds his way alone. He wanders in the wilderness for years trying to find his way out. Even more rarely does he take the way when he finds it, unless God sends someone to urge him along. That's exactly where the church is today. We need to be prodded by some man of God in the direction that God wants us to go. Joshua and Caleb were God's men to prod Israel to go into the promised land.

I like what it says in Joshua 6:12: "Joshua rose early in the morning" to carry out God's commands. He had no hesitation because he trusted God and believed that God would be true to His word.

Have you ever noticed in the Scriptures that the great souls were always eager, even when obedience was extremely hard? I think of the story of Abraham and Isaac and how Abraham arose early in the morning to go to the mountain that God was leading them to. Abraham had waited a long time for Isaac to be born. Isaac came when both Abraham and Sarah were well beyond the years of bearing children. They had the patience to wait upon God's blessing.

Sometimes the delayed blessing is the greatest blessing we can experience. The delay in getting a son was not due to

Abraham's disobedience but to God's providence. As far as God is concerned, timing is an important part of our walk. But we get impatient and try to get ahead of His timing.

Israel's delayed blessing was the result of disobedience, not wanting to do what God called them to do. Again, timing is important.

Sometimes the delayed blessing is the greatest blessing we can experience.

An essential lesson here is that a delayed blessing is still God's blessing. God is not intimidated by our disobedience. But just like Israel, we will pay dearly for our disobedience, and God will still have His way in the end.

What do you think is the greatest disappointment for Jesus? Modernism, blindness in churches, or languor in the hearts of those who know the truth? He is disappointed in those who know the way to go but have refused to go in that direction.

Thank God that Joshua rose early in the morning. He was ready and anxious to complete God's work that was set before him.

It is vital that we go God's way and receive His atonement and mercy, but almost everyone is wandering in the wilderness. We sing, "Is not this the land of Beulah," but what do the facts reveal?

They had to wade into the Jordan River, and only after that did the waters part. That was courage, faith, and cooperation on their part. The water was there, and when they put their feet into the water it parted.

Too many people wait for the removal of all obstacles. They wait for a miracle or providence to smooth the way for them. But Israel stepped into the water, and after they stepped in, the water parted.

As Christians obey and cross the river, even if it looks like they are drowning, they count on God to do His part. And then they take that wonderful leap of faith.

You have floundered for years. You have stood at the barrier to the blessed land for a long time, but it's time to rise up. The Lord of all nature commands you.

▼

Is Not This the Land of Beulah?

I am dwelling on the mountain,
    Where the golden sunlight gleams
O'er a land whose wondrous beauty
    Far exceeds my fondest dreams;
Where the air is pure, ethereal,
    Laden with the breath of flow'rs,
They are blooming by the fountain,
    'Neath the amaranthine bow'rs.

Is not this the land of Beulah?
Blessed, blessed land of light,
Where the flowers bloom forever,
And the sun is always bright!

Attributed to William Hunter
(1811–1877)
and Harriet Warner Re Qua
(dates unknown)

20

Appreciating
the Crisis Experience

▼

Heavenly Father, my journey forward is one of absolute faith. My faith in Thee is what drives me step-by-step. I praise Thee for Thine encouragements along the way. If it were not for Thee, I would have failed a long time ago. Thy faithfulness to me has encouraged my faithfulness to Thee. I praise Thee for getting me through some very difficult times. If left to myself, I certainly would have gone down the wrong path. I also believe, O Lord, that Thou art in charge of my next steps. I'm not sure where Thou wilt take me, but I'm sure Thou wilt take me down the right path. Forgive me for making my own decisions about the direction of my life. Thank Thee for keeping me in the right path. I pray this in the name of the Lord Jesus Christ, amen.

srael, now under the leadership of Joshua, prepared to cross the Jordan and go into the promised land. A sharp line had been drawn, which is why the ark of the covenant stood in the midst of the Jordan on dry ground. Once they crossed that line, they were never to go back.

> And the priests that bare the ark of the covenant of the Lord stood firm on dry ground in the midst of Jordan, and all the Israelites passed over on dry ground, until all the people were passed clean over Jordan.
>
> Joshua 3:17

They crossed the line, and the people of Israel experienced a crisis. It was a memorable event to say the least. They were finally getting to the place where God wanted them to be, which is always a crisis experience, but does not warrant going backward.

I believe this is the way God works. We can see it in creation where God created the heavens and the earth and there was no going back. The fall of man in the garden of Eden was also a crisis experience from which Adam and Eve could not go backward.

This is true in the human experience—birth and death and even conversion. These all are points of our lives that cross a particular line, and we cannot go backward after crossing it.

The filling of the Holy Spirit is not some casual experience we can take or leave. There is a spiritual line to be crossed—a crisis experience—that brings us into God's promised land.

Following this crisis come growth and development, and with those come conquests of the lands around us. Once we cross that spiritual line, we then begin a new experience that can only be engineered by the work of the Holy Spirit in a life that has been surrendered to Him.

As Joshua led the people across the Jordan, he was leading a surrendered people who were going to experience things they had never experienced before.

There are always reasons behind everything God does or leads us to do. In Joshua 4, we read how the Lord told Joshua to set up twelve stones as a monument to show that the twelve tribes of Israel had crossed a particular line and were never to go back again.

We need to have markers that remind us of what God is doing in our lives and how God is leading us to cross a particular line and never go back. This is an individual thing for the most part. But even for a congregation there are markers we must establish to remind us of how God is leading us and that God does not want us to go backward, but forward in the power of the Holy Spirit.

We need to have markers that remind us of what God is doing in our lives.

Joshua's monument of twelve stones was to inspire the next generation. Whenever they saw it, fathers would explain to their children how God led them, how God brought them across the Jordan, how God established their future but they had to turn their back on their past. Sometimes we get so caught up with the past that we cannot see what God is doing right now. This monument was to remind them to keep going forward and not to look back.

I think I am safe in saying that we have too much unclear Christianity today, if it can really be called Christianity. So much in our Christianity has no clear meaning to it. We have so mingled with the culture that it is hard to distinguish between the two. There is no hard line drawn between the world and Christianity today.

Somebody visits a church and sees an old friend, comes up to him, and says, "Hi, Bill. I didn't know you went to church. I didn't even know you were a Christian."

What I want to emphasize is the fact that the true Christian is known. There is no question about that person being a Christian.

It is similar to the birth of a baby. We know that baby has been born because there it is right in front of us. No question about it.

The same goes for that Christian who has been born again. The spiritual experience is real. There is the struggle, the pain, and the labor, and finally we come into the sunlight of God's redeeming power.

There are some reasonable conclusions I want to state here.

If we do not know that we have crossed a line, we have not. If we do not know when, we have not. An experience is the reality of crossing that line.

I believe it is the same with other aspects of our Christian experience.

If you do not know that you have consecrated yourself to the Lord and do not know when, you probably have not consecrated your life unto the Lord.

If you do not know when you surrendered to the Lord, you have not surrendered.

If you do not know when you were filled with the Holy Spirit, you were not filled with the Holy Spirit.

These personal experiences are landmarks in our walk with Christ. Just as the Israelites had that monument reminding them of crossing the Jordan, so we have monuments reminding us of experiences with Christ. Our conversion, our filling with the Holy Spirit, our surrender to Christ are all landmarks and monuments to our encounters with Him.

Nobody will go to heaven who does not know now that they are going to heaven. It is not guesswork; it is the reality of the personal experience that makes us completely confident in our walk with Christ. Joshua 5:1 says,

> And it came to pass, when all the kings of the Amorites, which were on the side of Jordan westward, and all the kings of the Canaanites, which were by the sea, heard that the Lord had dried up the waters of Jordan from before the children of Israel, until we were passed over, that their heart melted, neither was there spirit in them any more, because of the children of Israel.

The people's fright is not surprising. In Joshua 4:24, God promised that "all the people of the earth might know the hand of the Lord" through His actions, "that ye might fear the Lord your God for ever." For some reason the inhabitants of the land understood they were up against an enemy they could not handle.

In our Christian experience, as we cross the line God has set for us, we will find out that our obstacles begin to melt.

They cannot stand up against the fiery leading of the Holy Spirit in our lives. When we look at them in the beginning they look ferocious and unbeatable, but as we obey God, surrender ourselves to Him, and cross that line He has for us, those obstacles start to disappear. It is not that they cannot stand against us—they cannot stand against the God who is leading us in the direction He wants us to go.

As we walk in His direction, we begin to experience victories. We win victories day after day after day, and God directs us through this land of promise and the victories that come our way.

Nothing is more evident of my experience with God than the obstacles before me melting and the victories I am winning in the name of Jehovah.

It is one thing to say you are surrendered, but it is another thing to have the evidence as well as the witnesses of your surrender to Christ. You cannot surrender to Christ and have nobody notice it.

What about clear evidence of your detachment from the world? We need to be detached from the world, and not just in word only—it has to be in deed. Then those around us will notice a difference in our lives and a severe separation from the world around us.

Then I want a clear witness of your crossing over the Jordan into the promised land. Where are those witnesses who will corroborate your testimony of walking across the Jordan and possessing the land God has for you?

The challenges before us are the battles we have to engage in, which represent what the deeper life is all about. God is guiding us, and the path He has established contains battles. These battles are the pathway to victory.

▼

On to Victory

Christian, gird the armor on,
   There's a vict'ry to be won
   For the Lord, for the Lord;
Take the helmet, sword, and shield,
   Forth unto the battlefield
   At His Word, at His Word.

On we'll march to victory;
   Jesus will our leader be,
   Jesus will our leader be;
On we'll march to victory,
   To a final and a glorious victory.

Elisha A. Hoffman (1839–1929)

21

Getting Established in the Land of Promise

▼

My blessed Holy Spirit, thank Thee so much for Thy faithfulness in leading me down the pathway to the land of promise. I acknowledge I have had some troubling times, which were a result of not truly trusting. Forgive me, O Holy Spirit, for doubting Thee and trying to discover things in my own strength. I praise Thee for the wonderful way in which Thou hast led me. I praise Thee that my faults and failures in no way compromise Thine ability to lead and direct me. Thank Thee so much for Thy patience with me. I pray, O Holy Spirit, that Thy patience may be reflected through my life as I try to be patient with other believers. May Thy grace and power be my strength day by day. In Jesus' precious name I pray, amen.

srael is in the promised land, and with the past behind them, they are going forward under the leadership of Joshua. The pillar—the monument of twelve stones—was set up, and they are taking possession of the land.

There are three results of setting up the pillar and establishing themselves in the land.

The first is found in Joshua 5:2–9, where Israel was circumcised.

Circumcision was the mark of God on His people and had a long history with the Israelites. It began with God's command to Abraham: "This is my covenant, which ye shall keep, between me and you and thy seed after thee; Every man child among you shall be circumcised" (Genesis 17:10).

After Israel came out of Egypt, it was renewed under Moses. During their time in Egypt, they did not practice this rite of circumcision. Before God could allow them into the promised land, they had to renew this vow unto Jehovah.

Circumcision was the sign of God on His people that they were different from the other inhabitants of the land. God's people are always separate from the world around them.

The implication of this is that circumcision rolled away the reproach of Egypt from Israel. They could not come into Canaan with any of the Egyptian effects on them. They had to be completely separated from everything Egyptian.

The application to us today is that God has separated us from the world around us. Our conversion is our spiritual circumcision that separates us from the world. If my conversion is not separating me from the world around me, it is not a genuine conversion. What reason is there for conversion if it is not as drastic as circumcision?

God's people are always separate from the world around them.

How many people have what I call an artificial conversion? In other words, not a real biblical conversion to Christ. It is one thing to improve your life and clean it up a bit, but it is another thing to be transformed by the power of God. Conversion is being transformed, not merely updated.

People can clean up their lives, break their old habits, and begin new habits that are beneficial to their health, but that is not a biblical conversion. Real conversion is the mark of God on your life, making you distinguishable from the world around you. If the world does not recognize that you are born again, you have not been born again.

The second result is the manna ceased (Joshua 5:10–12). All through the wilderness experience, God gave His people daily manna from heaven. Now that they had crossed the Jordan into the promised land, this provision ceased.

This was a sign of Israel's maturing in their walk with God. The manna had only been temporary, as God's gift to Israel on a daily basis, but now that had ceased. God transferred them over to the fruits of Canaan, a more mature diet. What a change for Israel. Remember how at times they were tired of the daily manna and complained to God? That is how immaturity works. As they matured in their walk with God, He moved them to a much better food supply.

The fruit in Canaan was not a result of Israel planting trees. It was a result of Israel obeying God and following Him into that land. They took possession of the land, which included all of the fruit of Canaan.

We see this outlined for us in the New Testament with the Corinthian Christians (1 Corinthians 3:1–2), and then with the Hebrew Christians (Hebrews 5:11–14).

The purpose of coming into Canaan was to move Israel into a state of maturing in the things of God. That was the whole purpose, and for us today we are challenged by God to grow in the things of God. This is the great problem with today's Christians. They are living as if they were still in the wilderness, still eating manna; they have not acclimated to the fruit of Canaan.

Today we hear the cry, "I want something to do. I'm bored." So we supply churchgoers with fiction and drama and all kinds of entertainment. In the gospel church today, there is as much entertainment as there is out in the world.

The average Christians today, or I should say those who think they are Christians, do not know the difference between entertainment with its roots in the world and the true worship of God. If they could only experience the true worship of God, they would never be satisfied with worldly entertainment.

The third result is the appearance of the Man with the sword (Joshua 5:13–15).

Here was the experience of a lifetime for Joshua. This Angel was truly the Holy Spirit encountering Joshua. He is the Comforter as described in the New Testament (John 14).

He gave an encouraging message to Joshua to go ahead and finish the work God had called him to do. There are times we need a fresh message of encouragement from the

Lord. What Joshua was going through qualified him for this kind of encouragement. How can you know you are doing what God wants you to do if you do not have an ongoing relationship with Him like Joshua experienced?

The land of Canaan was the land of worship. It was consumed with the worship of Jehovah.

It began with Abraham, Abram at the time, in Genesis 12:7–8. "And the Lord appeared unto Abram, and said, Unto thy seed will I give this land: and there builded he an altar unto the Lord, who appeared unto him. And he removed from thence unto a mountain on the east of Bethel, and pitched his tent, having Bethel on the west, and Hai on the east: and there he builded an altar unto the Lord, and called upon the name of the Lord."

Jacob built an altar: "And God said unto Jacob, Arise, go up to Bethel, and dwell there: and make there an altar unto God, that appeared unto thee when thou fleddest from the face of Esau thy brother" (Genesis 35:1).

Then Joshua loosed his shoes. Joshua 5:15 says, "And the captain of the Lord's host said unto Joshua, Loose thy shoe from off thy foot; for the place whereon thou standest is holy. And Joshua did so."

Canaan was a land of worship, and God directed His people in various forms of worship.

There is a land here on earth where the soul anoints its altar.

The question that must be asked is, Where are you? What is your Christianity? Is it social? Is it formal? Is it entertaining? Is it theological? Is it escapist?

Or is it Christianity that is worshipful and pleases God, filled with ecstasy and rapture in His presence?

▼

To Canaan's Land I'm on My Way

To Canaan's land I'm on my way,
Where the soul never dies;
My darkest night will turn to day,
Where the soul never dies.

No sad farewells,
No tear-dimmed eyes;
Where all is love,
And the soul never dies.

William M. Golden (1878–1934)

22

When Discouragement Strikes, Be Encouraged

Gracious heavenly Father, I beseech Thee at this time to comfort my heart and soul. Many things have caused me to become discouraged and have deflected my attention from Thee. I find myself in the slough of despond. O my God, forgive me for allowing circumstances to take my focus off Thee. Help me to see that in my discouragement are opportunities to discover more of Thy grace and mercy. Lead me, Holy Spirit, in the paths that will bring rejoicing to my heart. Allow me to use my discouragement to rejoice in Thee. I ask this, O Father, in Jesus' name, amen.

Many believe once they become Christians and get into Canaan, there will be no more discouragement. Everything will be fine, uplifting, and joyful. I wish that were so, but it really is not.

However, I want to emphasize that discouragement, although it has a very negative effect on our lives, can have a positive effect.

We can become discouraged, but in that discouragement, we begin to see two things. First, our own weakness, and second, how God's grace is applied to our lives in that weakness.

Discouragement can easily become a ruling emotion. It becomes an outlook and attitude and the lens through which we see everything.

A farmer on a rainy day looks out the window and sees all of that rainy weather. All he sees out there is the rain, and it is a moody kind of an atmosphere. However, that weather is what the field needs to determine if it will have a good crop and what kind of plants will grow. The farmer looks beyond the moody, rainy weather and sees the crops.

A person's mood does not define him or her, but it can determine whether there will be good times or bad times. Just like in the farmer's field, it cannot be sunny every day of the week. That would compromise the crop. We cannot expect every day to be free from the things that foster moodiness. We cannot think that we will never experience discouragement.

Discouragement always plays on self-pity. At any gathering there will be Christians who are bothered by some degree of discouragement. Where that discouragement comes from can be anywhere. But it does come, and it changes our mood and our outlook on everything.

This is where the enemy is delighted. The more discouraged we are, the more delighted he is, and he focuses on those things that will feed into our discouragement.

And there are people who are suffering from so deep a discouragement that it affects them physically.

Many times these people put on an act. They are deeply discouraged and full of discontent, but they hide it from everybody. They have learned to smile and look happy, but if you could get at the root of their lives you would find they are deeply discouraged and discontented. Many have bought into the idea that a Christian should never get discouraged. If they get discouraged, they do not want anybody to know it.

What causes discouragement, particularly among Christians?

The difference between negative thinking and positive thinking is that negative thinking finds out what is wrong and positive thinking decides how to fix it. The doctor's diagnosis tells you what is wrong and what to do about it.

One of the causes of discouragement can be seen in the life of Elijah. He is a dramatic example of a man who became deeply discouraged because there was nobody around him who was going his way. Everybody seemed to have abandoned him. He lacked a like-minded soul.

You may be experiencing the same thing. Whether it's in your home, office, or some other part of your life, you have no like-minded soul with whom to fellowship.

154

Now, that may benefit you as it did Elijah. Here is a little trick I want to tell you. It was when Elijah stood by himself and all the other prophets had abandoned him that he showed the world around him what God could do in the face of Baal.

There is a saying that goes, "The bigger it is, the harder it falls." It is the same in the spiritual world.

Some Christians are never discouraged because they never had much to begin with. They do not expect anything, and when they do not get it, they just say, "Well, that's okay."

But there are Christians with higher ideals—higher than they are able to reach. After six months of struggling, if they can't reach them, they turn their back on them in discouragement. The loftier the spiritual aspiration, the deeper they go into the swamp of discouragement. John Bunyan called it the Slough of Despond in his book *The Pilgrim's Progress*.

But what is the cure?

Discouragement is based on an erroneous belief. The error is simply that you think you are alone when actually you are not. In the first place, there are many like you. Your discouragement is also based on not remembering that God is with you and that you are never alone. What kind of God would God be if He did not send His Angel to go before us?

I know there are times that we are in a tight spot. Even our Lord was in a situation where His sweat was like great drops of blood, and then an angel came and ministered unto Him. It was when Elijah was in deep discouragement that God sent him an angel to go down and bake a cake for him.

Many Christians are discouraged by the wickedness of the people around them.

We have Jeremiah, known as the weeping prophet, as another example. Everywhere he looked was wickedness. They had no newspapers in that day, but if they did, he would say most of the paper was covered with wickedness or reports of wicked means or wicked ideas. Jeremiah got it, but nobody else was paying any attention. He may be called the weeping prophet, but he was a long way from being discouraged (Lamentations 3:24).

The saint always stands out when darkness rises upon the earth.

What are you going to do about your discouragement? Remember, the stars in heaven do not shine in the daytime; it is already light upon the earth. Why do they shine at night? Because the darkness makes them visible. So in all the periods of history the saint always stands out when darkness rises upon the earth.

Instead of being discouraged, pray something like this, "Father, I thank Thee that though I am not as great as the great souls of the past, I know Thou canst work through me in any circumstance."

So remember this when going through discouraging times: The Lord God will help us through the Angel that is before us, and therefore we shall not be discouraged, but rather our encouragement will be in Him.

If you have been coming to shadows and darkness, and if you been trapped by the devil, you have the perfect right to stand up and say, "The Lord God will help me; therefore shall I not be confounded" (Isaiah 50:7). To all who walk in darkness and have no light, trust in the name of the Lord. Put yourself upon God, and you will be all right (see Isaiah 42:16).

Be Not Afraid

"Be not afraid, 'tis I,
Be not afraid, 'tis I";
Though wild winds blowing,
My bark o'erflowing,
God rules in earth and sky:
"Be not afraid, 'tis I,
Be not afraid, 'tis I";
The storm can't harm my trusting soul,
For Jesus walks the waves that roll;
His voice I hear, which calms my fear,
"'Tis I, be not afraid."

Barney Elliott Warren (1867–1951)

23

Piercing the Clouds of Concealment

▼

God and Father of our Lord Jesus, we thank Thee that Thou hast not allowed us to wander in the serpent-infested valley and abandoned us there. But Thou hast allured and wooed us and even placed a door in front of us. Wherever we are, there is a way out and a way in. Thou hast arranged it in Thy grace. Thou hast sent Thy Son, Jesus, to die, to rise, to live, and to be for us an advocate above. We bless Thee. We will not despair, we will not give up, we will not surrender to the enemy. We will dare to believe that with every temptation Thou hast made a way that will turn our tin into silver and our silver into gold and that Thou wilt give us the garments of praise for the garments of heaviness. Bless these words, we ask, in Jesus Christ our Lord, amen.

As we walk through Canaan, we are walking under the cloud by day and the fire by night. We are under God's protection, which includes every possibility, day and night. There is nothing that could ever happen to us that God has not prepared us for.

This Angel before us is leading us under the divine cloud God has provided. We have nothing to fear, knowing that we are going in the direction God wants us to go and that God's provisions are infinite.

When we face trouble, we do not have to give up. We know that there is a door of hope in the valley of despair. If there's trouble in your business, don't give up. If your nerves are frayed and you feel like a breakdown is just around the corner, don't you give up. Don't give up no matter what. For God says there's a door if you will only believe.

This idea of a door was supported by our Lord when He said, "I am the door: by me if any man enter in, he shall be saved, and shall go in and out, and find pasture" (John 10:9).

When we think about doors, we need to understand that there are some evil doors and there are some blessed doors.

I have visited prisons, and I think one of the most chilling sounds to be found anywhere on earth is the creaking of a prison door closing. The great lock being turned is distressing. So there are evil doors all around us.

But there are blessed doors as well. Sometimes these doors are not evident until we face some very difficult and discouraging times. God has the door there, but we don't see it until He is ready for us to see it.

The door opens into new territory. God built a door of hope so we would not despair when overwhelmed by our difficulties.

There is nothing that could ever happen to us that God has not prepared us for.

Remember, the blood of Jesus Christ cleanses us from all sin. He beckons to us: "And the Spirit and the bride say, Come. And let him that heareth say, Come. And let him that is athirst come. And whosoever will, let him take the water of life freely" (Revelation 22:17).

Jesus said, "Come unto me, all ye that labour and are heavy laden, and I will give you rest. Take my yoke upon you, and learn of me; for I am meek and lowly in heart: and ye shall find rest unto your souls" (Matthew 11:28–29).

There comes a time when we need to stop and say, "It looks as if there is no place to go from here." Okay, look straight ahead. There's the door, a door of hope that God has opened especially for you. Enter and you will find all joy and everything you need.

So we have provision as we are led by this Angel who is before us, and we need to embrace it with all the strength we have.

Take this truth to heart that God's smiling face is turned toward us. Don't let anybody sow seeds of doubt concerning this.

If that is so, and it is, why then do we not enjoy being Christians? Why then do we as Christians not share the wondrous divine illumination of the Savior Jesus Christ? Why do we not feel the divine fire in our hearts? Why do we not strive to sense and experience the feeling of reconciliation with God?

Why is it that the candles of our souls do not burn more brightly even now?

The reason is simply because there is between us and the smiling face of God a cloud of concealment.

How can we describe this cloud of concealment? We don't often hear this topic being discussed. It is this cloud that we allow to be over us, concealing from us the joy and wonder and awe of God's face shining on us.

This cloud of concealment can be a lot of things for the Christian.

There is the cloud of pride, for instance. You are your Father's child and heaven is your home, yet for a lifetime you may go without feeling the divine fire in your heart or experiencing the feeling of reconciliation with God. This can lead to moments of discouragement.

The devil will try to tell us, "God hates you. God has turned His back on you."

But God has never turned His back on any of His children since the hour Jesus groaned and died on the cross and said, "It is finished" (John 19:30). If we believe the devil's lie, we are under the shadow of that cloud.

The face of God is always turned our way, but if we allow this cloud of stubbornness we will not see His face. Some people are just plain obstinate and will not bend. They will not kneel to man or God or to anybody except the law. God declared to Israel, "Thy neck is an iron sinew, and thy brow brass" (Isaiah 48:4). He couldn't get them to yield because of their stubbornness.

The face of God is also concealed when we allow a cloud of self-will to come between us. Self-will can become a religious thing and enter right into church with you when you go to pray. Self-will is good-natured only when it's getting its own way, and it's grouchy and ill-tempered when it is crossed.

Then there is the cloud of ambition. You know there are even religious ambitions. There are people with religious ambitions for something that perhaps isn't in the will of God or that's for self-aggrandizement. And the result is a cloud between them and their God.

This cloud can be ambitions, stubbornness, self-will, pride, and anything else the Holy Spirit may point out to you. Only you know what it is. As a jealous lover, God will suffer no rival. Whatever rival there is, it is a cloud between us and God.

Some of you dear Christians have been walking under a cloud for a long time. You cannot get above it; you just cannot because you tried to pray your way above it. But it does not work that way. You must put it under your feet, rise above it, put all these things between you and all the creatures God ever made, and look away to the sunlight. Then relax, for there is nothing you can do. What can a person do? He cannot fill himself with the Holy Ghost, and he cannot cleanse his own heart. God has to do it, and He is anxious to do it, if we can use the word *anxious* when speaking about God. However, as much as God is on our side, He may wait before clearing the cloud that troubles us.

Meanwhile, we sit back, discouraged. We have been to so many altars and read so many books, and still the cloud hovers.

Dare to put the clouds of concealment under your feet and look into the sunshine to the Lord Jesus, not trying to tell Him what to do or how to do it. Just look on Him and let Him work.

▼

I Take, He Undertakes

I clasp the hand of love divine,
I claim the gracious promise mine,
And this eternal countersign,
"I take"—"He undertakes."

I take Thee, blessed Lord,
I give myself to Thee;
And Thou, according to Thy word,
Dost undertake for me.

Albert B. Simpson (1843–1919)

Notes

Chapter 4: Trusting the Holy Spirit to Lead Us

1. Raymond Bernard Blakney, trans., *Meister Eckhart: A Modern Translation* (New York: Harper & Row Publishers, Incorporated, 1941), 22, https://archive.org/details/in.ernet.dli.2015.65849.

Chapter 8: A Prepared Place for a Prepared People

1. William R. Newell, *Romans Verse-by-Verse* (Grand Rapids, MI: Kregel Publications, 1994), 82, https://books.google.com/books?id=JjkeUIl7jBwC.

A.W. Tozer (1897–1963) was a self-taught theologian, pastor, and writer whose powerful words continue to grip the intellect and stir the soul of today's believer. He authored more than forty books. *The Pursuit of God* and *The Knowledge of the Holy* are considered modern devotional classics. Get Tozer information and quotes at www.twitter.com/TozerAW.

Reverend James L. Snyder is an award-winning author whose writings have appeared in more than eighty periodicals and fifteen books. He is recognized as an authority on the life and ministry of A.W. Tozer. His first book, *The Life of A.W. Tozer: In Pursuit of God*, won the Reader's Choice Award in 1992 by *Christianity Today*. Because of his thorough knowledge of Tozer, James was given the rights from the A.W. Tozer estate to produce new books derived from over 400 never-before-published audiotapes. James and his wife live in Ocala, Florida. Learn more at www.jamessnyderministries.com.

More Practical and Powerful Resources by A.W. Tozer and James L. Snyder

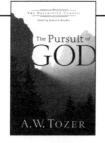
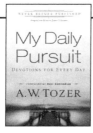
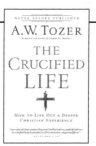
BETHANYHOUSE

 Stay up to date on your favorite books and authors with our free e-newsletters. Sign up today at bethanyhouse.com.

 facebook.com/BHPnonfiction   @bethany_house_nonfiction

 @bethany_house

Also by A.W. Tozer and James L. Snyder

This follow-up to *The Knowledge of the Holy* expounds on Tozer's thoughtful insights and delves deeper into the life-changing attributes of our God.

Delighting in God

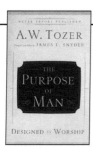

Tozer knew worship as the purpose of mankind and the expectation of God. This volume delivers Tozer's soul cry on worship and will inspire readers not only to understand worship but also to experience it in their own hearts.

The Purpose of Man

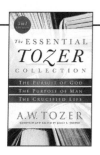

This 3-in-1 collection of A.W. Tozer's writings will strengthen your walk with Jesus. *The Pursuit of God* is sure to resonate if you long for a life spent in God's presence. *The Purpose of Man* is a call to worship as God reprioritizes your life and fills your soul. *The Crucified Life* will lead you to the cross so you can be raised to new life in Christ.

The Essential Tozer Collection

🛦 BETHANYHOUSE